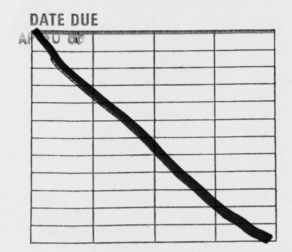

UNDERSTANDING
THE COLD WAR

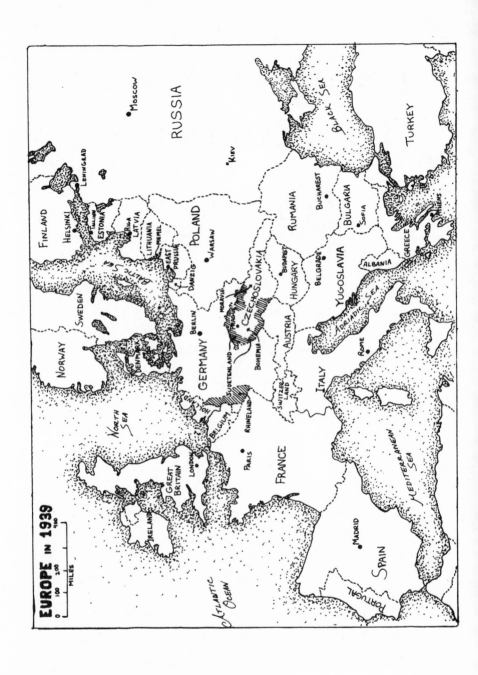

EUROPE IN 1939

MILES
0 100 200 400

ATLANTIC OCEAN

IRELAND

GREAT BRITAIN
London

NORTH SEA

NORWAY

SWEDEN

FINLAND

Helsinki

Leningrad

Moscow

RUSSIA

Kiev

ESTONIA
Tallinn

Riga
LATVIA

LITHUANIA
MEMEL

EAST PRUSSIA
DANZIG

POLAND
Warsaw

BALTIC SEA

DENMARK

GERMANY
Berlin

SUDETENLAND

MORAVIA
CZECHOSLOVAKIA
Prague

BOHEMIA

RHINELAND

BELGIUM

Paris

FRANCE

SWITZERLAND

ITALY

Rome

AUSTRIA

HUNGARY
Budapest

BELGRADE

YUGOSLAVIA

ALBANIA

ADRIATIC SEA

RUMANIA

Bucharest

BULGARIA
Sofia

GREECE

ATHENS

BLACK SEA

TURKEY

SPAIN
Madrid

PORTUGAL

MEDITERRANEAN SEA

UNDERSTANDING
THE COLD WAR

A Study of the Cold War
in the Interwar Period

Howard Roffman

RUTHERFORD • MADISON • TEANECK
FAIRLEIGH DICKINSON UNIVERSITY PRESS
LONDON: ASSOCIATED UNIVERSITY PRESSES

© 1977 by Associated University Presses, Inc.

Associated University Presses, Inc.
Cranbury, New Jersey 08512

Associated University Presses
Magdalen House
136–148 Tooley Street
London SE1 2TT, England

Library of Congress Cataloging in Publication Data

Roffman, Howard, 1953—
Understanding the cold war.

Bibliography: p.
Includes index
1. Russia—Foreign relations—1917–1945.
2. World politics—1919–1932. 3. World politics—
1933–1945. I. Title.
DK266.R594   327'.09'042   75–5251
ISBN 0-8386-1740-9

Also by HOWARD ROFFMAN:

Presumed Guilty: Lee Harvey Oswald in the Assassination of President Kennedy

PRINTED IN THE UNITED STATES OF AMERICA

Contents

Acknowledgments

I wish to thank the following publishers for having given me permission to quote from published works:

Atheneum Publishers, for permission to quote from A. J. P. Taylor, *The Origins of the Second World War.* Copyright © 1961 by A. J. P. Taylor. Reprinted by permission of Atheneum Publishers.

Houghton Mifflin Company, for permission to quote from Anthony Eden, *Facing the Dictators*, 1962.

Oxford University Press, for permission to quote from Issac Deutscher, *Stalin: A Political Biography*, 1949.

Praeger Publishers, Inc., for permission to quote from Adam B. Ulam, *Expansion and Coexistence*, 1968.

Macmillan & Co., Ltd. for British Commonwealth and world rights (excluding U.S.A.) to quote from E. H. Carr, *International Relations Between the Two World Wars, 1919–1939* (St. Martin's Press, 1947). Quoted by permission of Macmillan London and Basingstoke.

Martin Secker & Warburg Limited for British Commonwealth (excluding Canada) rights to quote from Adam B. Ulam,

Expansion and Coexistence (Praeger Publishers, Inc., 1968). Reprinted by permission.

Random House, Inc., for permission to quote from André Fontaine, *History of the Cold War*, vol. 1, 1968. Reprinted by permission of Pantheon Books, a Division of Random House, Inc.

St. Martin's Press, Inc., for permission to quote from E. H. Carr, *International Relations Between the Two World Wars, 1919–1939*, 1947.

This book was completed as my honor thesis in history during my undergraduate career at the University of Pennsylvania. I would like to express my thanks to my thesis advisers, Bruce Kuklick and H. M. Neiditch, for their valuable suggestions. I am especially grateful to my mother, Anita, without whose expert services as typist and secretary this book would not have been possible.

Introduction

The historical literature about the Cold War is vast and ever expanding. Numerous historians and analysts have offered their account of the breakdown of cooperation between the United States and the Soviet Union at the end of World War II. Yet, surprisingly few have examined Soviet Russia's relations with the West prior to World War II *in the context of the development of the Cold War.* Of all the histories of the Cold War, only a few include the period from the Bolshevik seizure of power in 1917 to the formation of the Grand Alliance in 1941. Although this twenty-four-year period has been described by historians in the context of the origins of the Second World War or the foreign policies of individual nations, no one has yet published a detailed analysis of this period, based on primary materials, from the point of view of the development of the Cold War. This is what I shall do in the following pages, with particular emphasis on the years 1937 to 1939.

The term *Cold War* has come to denote the conflict between Russia and the United States that developed at the end of World War II. Yet, the post-1945 Cold War cannot be properly understood except within the context of a much broader period of history. The *Cold War*, as I define it, is a conflict and hostility between the Soviet Union and the capitalist nations, particularly in the West, which proceeded from the very moment the Bolsheviks triumphed in Russia in 1917. In fact, for the three years following 1917, the Cold War was actually a "hot" war, during which foreign nations, including Japan, France, England, and the United States, sent troops and military aid to Russia to assist the anti-Bolshevik forces in the Russian civil war. During the interwar period, Russia and the West were engaged in a cold war, but Russia was in such a state of extreme weakness and domestic uncertainty that, at least until 1938, she was not a major diplomatic concern of the Western nations. With the coming of the Second World War, the Cold War went through several contrasting stages in rapid succession. In 1938 and 1939 the Cold War was waged between Russia, who sought to alter the status quo in Europe in her favor and against the designs of Hitler, and Britain and France, who sought to accommodate Hitler and thus effect changes in Europe unacceptable to Soviet interests and needs. When cooperation with Britain and France proved unattainable, the Soviets chose a temporary alliance with Hitler, which enabled the German dictator to attack Poland and thus start World War II. During the following two years, Russia was the nonmilitary ally of Britain's and France's enemy, and, indeed, the latter two almost went to war with the Soviets over Finland. When Hitler attacked Russia in the summer of 1941, an alliance mothered by necessity was formed among Britain, Russia, and, in a few months, the United States. The war completely changed the status quo in Europe and throughout the world. The United States replaced Britain as the paramount world power, and thus was left to face the second greatest world power at the end of the war, Soviet Russia. Russia, while suffering more devastation and human losses in the war than any other nation in any war in history, had established a military presence in Eastern Europe and was determined to maintain that area as her sphere of influence. Perhaps the central issue involved in the post-1945 phase of the Cold War was that of Soviet hegemony in Eastern Europe. The United States refused to accept a new status quo in which Soviet influence would be predominant among the nations of Eastern and Central Europe; ostensibly, the United States argued that the Soviets must allow the peoples of Eastern Europe to choose their own leaders and systems of government, and held this up as the price for postwar cooperation. As the Soviets seemed to grow stronger in their determination to control this area of Europe, U.S. policy proceeded on the assumption that Russia was a potential enemy, threatening American security. The Soviets, while at first willing to accept face-saving formulas in the shape of minor compromises and electoral façades, insisted on predominance in Eastern Europe as the sine qua non of postwar cooperation; they defended their position in terms of the needs of Soviet security and pointed out the failure of the West to allow democracy to function where it did not suit Western interests, such as in Greece, Spain, and Latin America.

No one has disputed Soviet security needs at the end of World War II. Russia had been invaded twice in 25 years through her geographically indefensible western frontier; if she were to be in a position to resist future invasions, she could not allow a return to the former status quo, that is, she would have to control the European corridor through which she had been invaded. Of course, many have argued that imperialistic or territorial aims and not concerns about security were what motivated the Soviet leaders at the end of the war, and that an expansionist-minded Russia posed a real threat to world peace. Some have argued that Russia's heavy-handed and anti-democratic means of securing her position in Eastern Europe, for whatever motives, left the West no choice but to oppose the expansion of Soviet influence in Europe.

The contemporary as well as the historical debate on this issue has been intense. Historians have devoted thousands of pages to analysis and exposition of the post-1945 Cold War in Europe. It is thus distressing that so little attention has been focused upon the pre-World War II Cold War in Europe, for the former cannot be properly understood without reference to the latter. Russia's position throughout and at the conclusion of World War II was directly related to the diplomacy that preceded the outbreak of the war, and her foreign policy in 1945 was doubtless very much influenced by her experiences leading up to her alliance with Britain and America. The United States was not in a comparable position in 1945, because she had had no major diplomatic dealings with Soviet Russia until the war. In the prewar years, Russia's principal antagonist in the Cold War was Britain; as a result of the war, the United States replaced Britain in this role. Thus, perhaps ironically, in dealing with the Soviet Union after 1945, the United States had to pay the price for Britain's prewar diplomacy. The situation was one that neither side could have avoided; Russia could not ignore the lessons of the past simply because she was now dealing with America instead of Britain, and the United States could not erase the consequences of a past policy for which she was not responsible.

In the following pages I will present an account of the diplomatic maneuverings of Britain and Russia in Europe during the interwar years, with particular emphasis on the period 1937 to 1939, when the most significant diplomacy took place. I would like the reader to understand that I have not attempted to analyze the origins of the Second World War or to describe, in a systematic or complete manner, the policies of Hitler and Mussolini. I am dealing with the interaction of Britain, France, and Russia in the context of the development of the Cold War. Within this framework it is often necessary to explain each country's foreign policy toward the fascist states, but only as it relates to the Cold War. This is particularly true in the case of Britain, whose policy under Neville Chamberlain was to accommodate Hitler's ambitions in Europe, which meant excluding Russia from European affairs and, in effect, assisting Hitler in his pursuit of a possible attack on Russia.

Chapter 1 provides a brief account of the years 1921 to 1936, the period that prefaced the important diplomacy of 1937 to 1939. The Russians emerged from their civil war in 1921 in a precarious domestic and foreign position; they faced mammoth tasks of reconstruction, virtually alone in a world of nations hostile toward their new government, so hostile as to have made a significant military contribution to the efforts to overthrow that government. The capitalist nations, particularly Britain, France, and the United States, all shared a profound distrust of the Bolsheviks and a deep fear of communism. Most of the governments in the West anticipated the downfall of the Bolshevik government in Russia, and feared that the example of a successful communist revolution in the world, in addition to the activities of the Comintern, spelled danger for the "democratic" way of life. Although the Cold War was a relatively insignificant factor in world politics during the period described in chapter 1, it was during this period that the foundations were laid for the time when relations between Russia and the West would profoundly affect the rest of the world: Soviet Russia successfully industrialized, Stalin secured his position as the uncontested leader of his country, Hitler came to power in Germany, the West experienced the economic chaos of the Great Depression, and the League of Nations, largely under Britain's lead, failed to preserve peace and instead became an instrument for the appeasement of fascism.

Chapter 2 begins with the coming to power of Neville Chamberlain as Prime Minister in 1937. In this chapter I will explain and analyze the great conflict between British and Soviet policies in Europe up to March 1939, when Hitler embarked on aggression of a new type. It will be necessary to describe and understand the infamous British "appeasement" policy. Although it is difficult to speak with equal assurance about Soviet policy because of the virtual absence of primary documentation from Soviet archives, I believe that it is possible to reach an understanding of the fundamental Soviet aims and intentions.

Chapter 3 closely examines the period from March to

August 1939. The Anglo-Soviet diplomacy of this period is of vital importance and, I believe, has not yet been adequately described or understood, especially within the context of the development of the Cold War. I will document how the Soviets put forth to Britain and France a serious proposal for an alliance to oppose Hitler and create a new European order that would recognize Soviet interests in Eastern Europe; how the British, still convinced of the necessity if not the rightness of appeasement, schemed to deny the Russians a place in Europe but still to use the shadow of Soviet power in a final effort to come to terms with Hitler; how Britain and France finally determined to resist German aggression by insuring that Eastern Europe and Russia would bear the burden òf fighting the Axis.

If there is a lesson in this story it is that the highest morality of international politics is that of national self-interest. Britain felt it in her interest to appease Hitler, to keep Soviet Russia out of Europe, and to make sure that other nations, particularly in the east, would eventually absorb the fury of Hitler's war machine. Such cold calculations, while they may offend the delicate morality of critics, defenders, and scholars, are the realities with which national governments must deal in protecting their countries. It is ironic that Britain's interwar leaders, particularly Chamberlain, who spoke endlessly of moral displays and missions, created for themselves a situation in which traditional morality would have to be almost wholly sacrificed to the pursuit of basic self-interest. Russia's policy was also dictated by self-interest, but it is a tragedy, or at least an irony, of history that the Chamberlain government did not fully realize that the British shared a common interest with the Russians in opposing Hitler. The British suffered from a stubborn blindness in dealing with the Soviets, and failed to recognize that the Russians, too, could have national interests so great that their achievement involved the question of national survival or destruction. The point is that, although British and Soviet perceptions of their respective vital interests were almost irreconcilable, it was the Soviet perception that was the more realistic.

Of course, it is impossible to say what would have happened had the British followed a different policy; what *did* happen was that a world war ensued in which the Russians paid by far the highest price in blood and devastation. Prior to the war they insisted that they would not pay such a price simply to preserve a European status quo that was stacked against them, but Britain and France refused to agree to a change in Europe that recognized or permitted Soviet predominance in Eastern Europe. When Russia was finally forced to fight Hitler, she again made it known that she was doing so not to preserve the old order; at the end of the war she was finally in a position to guarantee that she received what she felt was her due.

In this way were the contours of the postwar world shaped by the diplomacy of prewar Europe.

UNDERSTANDING
THE COLD WAR

1

The Ground Is Broken

The period from the end of civil war in Russia in 1921 until the rise of Hitler in Germany in 1933 is of limited significance in understanding the development of the Cold War. Russia was virtually isolated in the world and the governments of the West, seeing "the specter of Bolshevism in every sign of unrest, political or social," [1] feared both the example of a successful communist revolution in Russia and the clandestine, over-estimated activities of the Comintern. Yet, Russia's utter prostration after the civil war guaranteed that for some time she could not possibly be a formidable military threat to the status quo in Europe.

There can be no question that in the decade following the civil war Russia had to pursue a defensive foreign policy to counteract the "capitalist encirclement" that came about as a

1. Sumner Welles, *The Time For Decision* (New York: Harper and Brothers, 1944), p. 312.

19

result of Brest-Litovsk, Versailles, and Riga. After seven years of war, the country was virtually devastated and its economy was in a state of collapse. In the midst of reconstruction, a long power struggle ensued after Lenin's death in 1924. Adam Ulam has described the essential and paradoxical principles behind the foreign policy of Soviet Russia in the 1920s:

> On the one hand, the Soviet Union more than any large state required peace and international stability, both political and economic. The amount of wartime destruction, both human and economic, had been greater in Russia than anywhere else. Time was required to heal the wounds. Normal and extensive commercial intercourse with foreign countries was required to bring in badly needed capital and foreign specialists. . . . On the other hand, general prosperity and stability diminished the prospects of Communism.[2]

When Lenin embarked on his New Economic Policy in 1921, he realized that the outbreak of world revolution on which he had long counted was not to be had in the near future. Perhaps he still genuinely believed that the success of the Bolshevik revolution in Russia depended, in the long run, on the overthrow of the capitalist governments of the world. The Comintern remained ostensibly the organ of world revolution, but by the end of 1921 its power and real purpose were debatable. Lenin was a realist as much as he was a communist, and he was far more inclined to be persuaded by immediate needs than by theories of long-range needs. Thus there can be little doubt that what Russia needed most in 1921—peace, international stability, and economic cooperation with the West—is what Lenin wanted the most, and the goal of world revolution or weakening through subversion of the capitalist nations *had* to be relegated to second place.

Whatever the true role of the Comintern at this time, two facts are undeniable: (1) Comintern policy was a failure in that it did not produce a single revolution anywhere in the

2. Adam B. Ulam, *Expansion and Coexistence* (New York: Praeger, 1968), pp. 133–34.

world,[3] and (2) the very existence of the Comintern was an irritant in East-West relations; it was perceived by the capitalist nations as a threat against them, often seemingly without realistic consideration of its capabilities and powers. At the very least, its presence was regarded as an intrusion by Moscow into the affairs of other nations. Western nations repeatedly lodged formal protests in Moscow against the Soviet Union's use of subversive "propaganda" abroad; the halting of such "propaganda" was usually a condition stipulated by the capitalists in negotiations with the Russians about credits and recognition.[4]

The greatest foreign-policy coup under Lenin was the 1922 treaty of cooperation with Germany, Europe's leading industrial nation. The European powers had met in Genoa in 1922 with the intention of working together to reconstruct Europe's economy. The Soviet Union was invited to participate, but it was apparent that she was expected to do so only on Western terms, and her delegates "were isolated as if they were lepers."[5] Chicherin, representing Russia, and the German Foreign Minister, another outcast at the conference, met at Rapallo on Easter Sunday and negotiated a treaty establishing diplomatic relations, most favored trade status, and mutual assistance in economic matters. Economically, the two nations had mutual aims and interests; yet politically, the treaty had far greater importance for the Soviets as a means "to prevent Germany from coalescing with the West against Russia." [6] According to George Kennan,

> For the Western Allies, Rapallo meant the forfeiture of the collaboration of Germany as a possible partner in a united Western approach to the problem of Russian Communism.[7]

3. Ibid., p. 160; Welles, p. 313; Alvin Z. Rubinstein, *The Foreign Policy of the Soviet Union* (New York: Random House, 1972), p. 84.

4. George F. Kennan, *Russia and the West Under Lenin and Stalin* (New York; New American Library, 1961), p. 189.

5. Welles, p. 312.

6. Issac Deutscher, *Stalin: A Political Biography* (London: Oxford University Press, 1949), p. 409.

7. Kennan, p. 211.

The Western Allies were soon to recoup their loss at Genoa. In October 1925, Britain, France, Belgium, Holland, and Germany signed the Locarno Pact, a mutual security agreement that guaranteed Germany's Western borders. The treaty was a blow to Russia. "Since she had been excluded from the negotiations, she interpreted the pact . . . as directed against herself."[8] In spite of the Treaty of Berlin, a nonaggression pact reaffirming Rapallo and signed by Russia and Germany on April 24, 1926, Locarno represented a fundamental defeat of Soviet diplomatic aims. According to Ulam, "Germany was no longer a partner in the struggle against the European status quo; she now could and did play the Soviet Union against the West, and her partnership with Russia was no longer the main element but only one of many in her foreign policy."[9]

Without Germany, Soviet Russia had to seek other means of preventing a Western coalition against her. Her geographic position was virtually untenable: "From the Arctic Ocean to the Black Sea, [Russia] was fronted by one hostile state after another," the infamous *cordon sanitaire*.[10] By the end of 1924, every major power except the United States had accorded diplomatic recognition to the Soviet Union. This, however, gave little assurance to Moscow. Her diplomatic relations with Britain, established in February of 1924 with the victory of that country's first Labour Cabinet, were broken off at the end of the year after exposure of alleged Soviet interference in British labor problems. The Labour Party was overwhelmingly voted out in October 1924, and the Conservative Party, whose hostility to Soviet Russia was well known and often voiced, remained in power for the next six years. At the same time, in France, "the successive governments did not hide their anti-Soviet prejudices."[11] Thus, by 1926, to ensure the security of Russia's Western frontier, Moscow sought, "in effect, to undermine the

8. André Fontaine, *History of the Cold War*, vol. 1 (New York: Vintage Books, 1968), p. 61.
9. Ulam, p. 159.
10. Fontaine, p. 48.
11. Ibid., p. 63.

French alliance system in Eastern Europe." [12] A treaty of friendship and neutrality was negotiated with Lithuania in 1926, as well as a trade agreement with Latvia in 1927. In 1928 treaties of nonaggression were signed with Poland, Rumania, and Estonia, and in February 1929, these nations collectively signed the East Pact in Moscow.[13]

At the end of 1927, Stalin emerged victorious from the power struggle in which Trotsky, Zinoviev, and Kamenov were expelled from the party. Stalin's "socialism in one country" officially acknowledged what was by then obvious: world revolution was not imminent, and the paramount concern of communist leaders was to assure the success of the Russian revolution. The sixth congress of the Comintern, meeting in 1928, openly identified the interests of communist movements around the world with the Soviet Union, although it still gave lip service to the imminence of revolution. According to Issac Deutcher,

> With even greater emphasis than hitherto, as if ignoring all the trumpets of the Comintern, [Stalin] made "socialism in one country" the supreme article of faith, obligatory not only in his own party but in the Comintern as a whole. . . . His diplomacy was feeling its way even more cautiously than before and continued to work on the assumption of Russia's prolonged isolation. There was an undeniable contradiction between his two lines of policy, the one he pursued in Russia and the one he inspired in the Comintern. It is easy to guess which of the two policies had the greater weight.[14]

On the surface, the conduct of Soviet foreign policy in the five years after Stalin's achievement of uncontested power is highly erratic and almost defies explanation in terms of rational or systematic goals. This was probably due to the peculiar mixing of domestic and foreign circumstances during this period. Russia was still isolated and insecure in the world; the policy of Rapallo

12. Rubinstein, p. 79.
13. Ibid.
14. Deutscher, p. 405; see also E. H. Carr, *International Relations Between the Two World Wars* (New York: Harper and Row, 1947), pp. 76–78.

did not prevent German realignment with the West, and Stalin had suffered a major defeat in China. All told, Stalin, at the end of 1927, suffered what George Kennan describes as "a sense of frustration" in dealing with the problem of the capitalist encirclement.

> It encouraged him to withdraw from the effort to conduct an active foreign policy and to devote himself in the ensuing years to the economic strengthening of the Soviet Union, to the development of Soviet military power, and to the consolidation of his own regime internally. The five years following 1927 might be called, in fact, a period of isolationism in Soviet foreign policy—a period of withdrawal from external affairs during which great internal changes were undertaken.[15]

The explanation of Stalin's foreign policy during this period lies in his own personality and his approach to the domestic problems of his country. To say the least, he was heavy-handed. He was a despot who had in mind the complete reorganization and modernization of a vast and backward society. His programs were radical: a five-year plan for rapid industrialization and the collectivization of the peasantry. His implementation of policy was brutal and uncompromising and aroused an opposition that he smashed with a ruthlessness and violence that shook the country. Stalin's attitude toward the outside world at this time was one of cynicism and skepticism, and the conduct of foreign affairs occupied little of his time. It was during this period that the West experienced the Great Depression, which made the capitalist nations more anxious to provide the only thing that Stalin wanted from them at the time: "imports of machine tools and capital goods." [16] Probably counting on the ultimate ruin of bourgeois states as a result of the depression, Stalin "did not hesitate during those years to abuse Russia's relations with the Western countries for his own domestic purposes." [17] This was

15. Kennan, p. 263.
16. Ibid., p. 266.
17. Ibid.

the standard practice of an authoritarian leader raising the foreign bogey to preserve himself in the midst of a severe domestic crisis. "A degree of hysteria, a spy and sabotage mania had to be part of the propaganda campaign designed to explain to the Russian people their vast sufferings." [18]

Stalin's almost total preoccupation with domestic matters and his cynicism about foreign affairs during this period further irritated the nations of the West and caused the Soviet leader to misunderstand the significance of events abroad. It was during this period that the Nazis, led by Hitler, triumphed in Germany. Stalin, who undoubtedly did not take time for careful and thoughtful analysis of international developments, apparently "was completely unaware of the significance and the destructive dynamism of nazism. To him Hitler was merely one of the many reactionary leaders whom the political see-saw throws up for a moment." [19] Stalin simply failed, at this time, to understand the difference between Nazism and Fascism, which he saw as "the militant organization of the bourgeoisie" based on an alliance with Social Democracy. [20] It was because of this fundamental misunderstanding that Stalin, through his Comintern policy, fatally split the German left and probably aided Hitler's rise to power. [21]

One of the results of Stalin's first five-year plan was that by 1932 Russia was in the midst of one of her worst economic and political crises, with many parts of the country struck by famine. The paramount concern of Soviet foreign policy by 1932 was to avoid war, for even if Stalin still did not understand Hitler, he could not help but be concerned by the reintegration of Germany into the European community and the more serious maneuverings of Japan in Manchuria initiated by the Japanese army on September 18, 1931. With the Japanese occupation of Manchuria, Moscow feared a war on its eastern front and, while it

18. Ulam, p. 266.
19. Deutscher, p. 406.
20. Ibid.
21. Kennan, pp. 270–75.

could not, at this time, realistically expect an attack by Germany alone or allied with the West, a strengthening of the Soviet political/diplomatic position in Europe became essential as a preparation in the event of war with Japan.

Although an actual and significant reformulation of Soviet policy was at least a year and a half in the future, the basis for the 1933–34 policy change lay in Stalin's diplomacy of 1932–33, when he sought through treaties to prevent both war with Japan and the untenable position that might have resulted had Germany allied with the major capitalist nations against Russia. Adam Ulam has described 1932 as "the bumper year for non-aggression treaties . . . when the U.S.S.R. signed non-aggression pacts with Finland, Estonia, Latvia, Poland, and France." [22] Formal diplomatic relations with the United States were established in November 1933. Furthermore, at the end of 1932, Litvinov proposed a nonaggression pact between Russia and Japan. At first the Japanese seemed receptive, but in February 1933, the Japanese Cabinet decided to withdraw from the League of Nations, indicating "the complete supremacy of the military and a fundamental defeat for the moderate elements in the country." [23] This was clearly a cause for alarm in Moscow; on August 9, 1933, the British Ambassador reported from Moscow that "their major fear is from Japan." [24]

After Hitler's accession to power in January 1933, Stalin was increasingly given cause for alarm over Germany. Hitler withdrew from the League and the disarmament conference, signed a nonaggression pact with Poland, rejected Moscow's proposals for a mutual Russo-German guarantee for the Baltic states, and openly advertised his anti-Bolshevism, an unmistakable appeal to the West. "The last months of 1933 and the beginning of 1934 mark, then, the agonizing reappraisal of Soviet foreign

22. Ulam, p. 209.
23. James E. McSherry, *Stalin, Hitler and Europe* (Cleveland: The World Publishing Co., 1968), pp. 5–6.
24. Ibid., p. 33.

policy that was due to bring about its most basic shift in tactics since 1921." [25]

From 1934 to 1936, as long as Hitler remained unarmed, "the worst danger of all" for Russia, according to Ulam, was "that of concerted capitalist action against the Soviet Union." [26] In 1934, Soviet Russia, faced with a volatile domestic situation, could not seriously contemplate fighting a war; with the immediate threat of war looming on her eastern front, Russia had to consider how she could consolidate and improve her position vis-à-vis Europe. Ulam, in describing Soviet aims in this dangerous situation, makes a fundamental error by implying that the Soviet position remained the same after 1936:

> For the immediate and foreseeable future, the Soviet aims were not the punishment of aggressors or the preparation of a grand military alliance against them, but the noninvolvement of the Soviet Union in a war. Not a crusade against fascism, but the sensible objective of sparing their sorely tried country a military conflict they secretly realized it could not afford—this was uppermost in the minds of Stalin and his colleagues. To do them justice, the Soviet leaders during the period 1934–39 never made a secret of this objective or tried to pretend that their detestation of fascism was greater than their desire for military noninvolvement.[27]

It is correct that the Soviet Union wished to avoid war; it is also correct, at least as of 1936, that the Soviet government probably realized it was not prepared for war. What seems incorrect, especially for the period after 1937, is the allegation that Stalin did not try to achieve "the preparation of a grand military alliance" against the fascist powers, particularly Germany. I will argue that once Germany rearmed, Stalin genuinely believed that the only effective means of controlling Hitler was the formation of a military alliance so awesome that Hitler

25. Ulam, p. 195.
26. Ibid., p. 225.
27. Ibid., p. 217.

would not dare to attack it or, in the unlikely event he should choose to attack, his defeat would be assured. If one must isolate a single reason for Stalin's failure to secure the military alliance he sought, it is this: Britain's leaders faced the decision of which dictator they would have to come to terms with to avoid war, and they chose wrong. The French, although more ambivalent than the British, were not free agents. From 1936 on, their foreign policy was virtually dictated by the British.

Stalin was not opposed to fascism for reasons of high morality, and he certainly did not seek to join forces against Hitler out of a desire to protect capitalism. He sought cooperation with the West against Hitler *only* to save his country and, possibly, himself. That Russia and the capitalist nations of the West would have to join forces to effectively oppose Hitler was inevitable, and Stalin knew it. One of the tragedies of the period was that the British leadership was too feeble to meet the challenge that Hitler posed.

A major change in Soviet foreign policy became apparent in 1934 when the Soviet Union joined the League of Nations. Soviet Foreign Minister Litvinov, who was essentially Stalin's spokesman at the League, became a symbol of Russia's advocacy of peace through collective security; "Peace is indivisible" was his constant appeal. Sumner Welles, former Under Secretary of State, has praised Litvinov's record in the League:

> When the Soviet Union entered the League, even the most obstinate were soon forced to admit that it was the only major power which seemed to take the League seriously. . . .[28] Litvinov became the foremost prophet of the basic principles underlying the Covenant of the League of Nations. . . . Unfortunately, he proved to be a prophet in the wilderness. His insistence that peace is indivisible fell on deaf ears. His demand that the Western powers join with the Soviet Union in recognizing the dangers inherent in the rearmament of Germany was disregarded. . . .[29] It should never be forgotten that the Soviet Union did not desert the League. It was the

28. Welles, p. 31.
29. Ibid., p. 320.

great powers which dominated the League in its later years that deserted the Soviet Union.[30]

Soviet policy in the League was but a part of Stalin's new diplomacy. Stalin was blunt in recognizing the severe limitations of the League; to him the world organization could serve only as a "brake" or time-buying device on aggression. Beginning during the summer of 1934, Litvinov took the initiative for an "Eastern Locarno," "pacts of mutual assistance" that would have joined France, the U.S.S.R., Russia's Western neighbors, Britain, and Germany in a treaty of nonaggression and mutual guarantees. France was interested, but German and Polish opposition doomed the plan.[31] Issac Deutscher writes that "by the beginning of 1935 Stalin had passed from the futile attempt at creating a regional, eastern European system of defense to plans for alliances with the West." [32] In March 1935, Stalin met with British foreign minister Anthony Eden in Moscow and warned of the dangers of Hitler and the need to form an alliance against him.[33] In May of the same year Russia signed treaties of mutual assistance with France and Czechoslovakia; these treaties were seriously limited by stipulated contingencies and the lack of any military protocol.[34] In July a nonaggression treaty with Poland was signed. These changes in diplomatic tactics, in which the Soviet government openly declared itself opposed to fascism as the primary threat to peace, necessitated a radical alteration of Comintern policy. At the seventh congress of the International in July and August of 1935, the old and grievously inaccurate dogma about fascism was quietly buried and a new line was adopted: "Social Democrats and Communists were called upon to join hands and form 'Popular Fronts' which were to include all middle-class parties and groups, Liberal and Radical, and

30. Ibid., p. 31.
31. Deutscher, pp. 417–18; Ulam, pp. 218–19; Carr, pp. 203–4.
32. Deutscher, p. 418.
33. Anthony Eden, *Facing the Dictators* (Boston: Houghton Mifflin Co., 1962), pp. 164–78.
34. Ulam, pp. 223–24.

even Conservative, who declared themselves willing to stand up against fascism." [35]

In the most skeptical view, Soviet diplomacy in the post-1933 period, involving endless oratorical tirades against fascism and unfulfilled calls for action in response to German and Italian aggression, was deceitful and misleading because, in the end, Russia would not have gone to war unless she was directly attacked. I would take issue with this point of view for two reasons: (1) It is a virtually pointless academic issue because the contingency never arose from 1934 to 1939, that is, the West never called Stalin's bluff by taking action against fascist aggression, and (2) it distorts the basic premises and aims of Stalin's policy.

Soviet diplomacy in the 1934–1939, and especially in the 1934–1936 period was based on two major premises: (1) A military alliance between Russia and the European powers against Germany and Italy would have been so awesome that Hitler would not have dared strike, especially in Eastern Europe, and (2) To underscore this alliance and to be prepared for the contingency that Hitler should decide on war, each nation in the alliance, particularly Russia, must increase its military strength.[36] There is ample evidence to substantiate my assertion

35. Deutscher, p. 419.
36. Ulam argues that "the original aim of the Popular Front tactics" from Stalin's point of view, "was not to provide the Western countries with the resolution and the material means to fight Hitler" (Ulam, p. 229). There is no evidence to support this view. When French Foreign Minister Laval visited Moscow in May 1935, he sought Stalin's support for France's armaments policy. Stalin was obliging, and a joint communiqué was issued expressing the Soviet leader's "complete understanding and approval of the national defense policy pursued by France with the object of maintaining its armed forces at a level consistent with its security requirements" (Ulam, p. 228). Ulam attempts to deny the obvious meaning of this statement by citing the "ambiguous" attitude of the French Communists toward rearmament and by making the assumption that "the policy of the French Communist Party was attuned to the wishes of Moscow." He fails to consider the domestic political situation in France and the real dilemma that Stalin's declaration posed for the French Communists.

that these factors were the cornerstones of Stalin's diplomacy.

In his first speech as the Soviet representative to the League, Litvinov broadly outlined a Soviet policy designed not to *make* war against fascism but to *prevent* the fascist powers from making war. "Now, the organization of peace, for which so far very little has been done, must be set against the extremely active organization of war." Litvinov admitted that, of all the delegates, he probably best realized the limitations of the League to organize for peace: "I am however convinced that, with the firm will and close cooperation of all its members, a great deal could be done at any given moment for the utmost *diminution of the danger of war*." [37] When Stalin met with Eden in March 1935, he said that "the only way to meet the present situation was by some scheme of pacts. Germany must be made to realize that if she attacked any other nation she would have Europe against her." [38] During the same visit, Litvinov was more explicit with Eden. He said:

> I do not regard mutual assistance as a real guarantee of defense, but rather as a deterrent; as a last resort the Soviet Union has to rely upon her own forces. But if Germany knew that she would find ranged against her a coalition composed of a number of states she might hesitate to risk her fate.[39]

Eden was shown an airplane factory at Fili where the Russians constructed large bombers. "It was clear," Eden later wrote, "that the Soviet authorities wished me to be impressed by this evidence of their ability to support any international assurances they might give." [40] On May 22, 1939, in the midst of negotiations between Britain, France, and Russia for a possible alliance (to be discussed in detail at a later point), the Soviet Ambassador in London, Maisky, told British Foreign Minister Halifax that the "essential thing was to prevent war. [The] Soviet government thought this could be done but only by organizing such a

37. Rubinstein, p. 127.
38. Eden, p. 173.
39. Ibid., p. 164.
40. Ibid., p. 178.

combination of forces that Germany would not dare to attack." [41]
According to Deutscher, Stalin's "military and diplomatic advisers were telling him, and they were not wrong, that at that stage [1935–1937] Germany's adversaries could stop Hitler, at least for a time, by the mere threat of military action." [42]

Stalin understood that the threat of a military alliance would be meaningless, indeed his whole foreign policy would be paralyzed, unless Russia were prepared for war. His first five-year plan was instituted with a view toward strengthening Russia's military power through rapid industrialization and the elimination of real or potential traitors. In the face of the threatening world situation of 1933–34, military preparations were vastly increased, as André Fontaine describes:

> In two years, military expenditures rose eight times, the number of men in the Red Army more than doubled and the number of airplanes increased from 2,500 to 4,000. Party control over the army was constantly strengthened. [43]

Furthermore, in a major reform during 1935–36, the Red Army was modernized and mechanized. [44] To be sure, Stalin's purge of 1936–1938, in which a majority of the top army leadership was eliminated, had the effect of causing Britain and France to view Soviet military potential with great skepticism and doubtless impaired to some degree the army's effectiveness (although the Soviet army's performance in conflicts with the Japanese during and after the purge was excellent). This matter will be discussed at a later point. The essential observation here is that Stalin *did* undertake the military preparations that would have made his proposed alliances against the Axis powers feasible and effective. As I will discuss later, neither a meaningful

41. E. L. Woodward et al., eds., *Documents on British Foreign Policy, 1919–1939*, third series (London: Her Majesty's Stationery Office), 5: 630–31. (Hereinafter referred to as DBFP.)
42. Deutscher, p. 421.
43. Fontaine, p. 80.
44. Deutscher, p. 421.

effort at rearmament nor an elementary understanding of the threat posed by Hitler was forthcoming from the British.

Stalin's alliance with France gave him a partial assurance that Germany could not form a European alliance against the Soviet Union, but on a relative scale it did little toward protecting Russia's security. Events in Britain and Germany were contributing to a far more threatening situation. In March 1935, in violation of the provisions of Versailles and Locarno, Germany decreed universal military service. Litvinov protested Germany's action in the League, where London and Paris were silent.[45] On June 18, 1935, Hitler signed a naval treaty with Great Britain. By this treaty, England gave its approval to Hitler's violation of the naval clauses of Versailles and actually provided for a contingency, *to be decided by Germany,* in which Germany could build up to a hundred percent of British submarine strength. In short, the effect of the treaty "was to authorize Germany to build to her utmost capacity for five or six years to come." [46] No other nation was consulted before the treaty was signed, a tactic that incensed France. Furthermore, it was an act of folly to *encourage* German rearmament when, for their own political reasons, the British cabinet was deliberately doing nothing worthwhile to prepare England militarily. Perhaps most incredible of all was that the British Admiralty could so soon forget the horrible experience of the First World War when German submarines had threatened to starve Britain out of the war, and only American aid had saved her. Now the isolationist sentiment in the U.S. Congress made such aid an unreliable prospect, yet, in the words of D. F. Fleming, "London cheerfully granted a maniacal German ruler with absolute power in his hands the right to build as many submarines as Britain had." [47]

The response to Mussolini's aggression against Ethiopia in

45. D. F. Fleming, *The Cold War and Its Origins,* vol. 1 (New York: Doubleday and Co., 1961): 54.
46. Winston S. Churchill, *The Gathering Storm* (Boston: Houghton Mifflin Co., 1948), pp. 137–42.
47. Fleming, p. 60.

1935 marked the virtual death of the League and provided a preview of the Anglo-French diplomacy of appeasement that would encourage Hitler's expansion in the next four years. At first the League voted sanctions against Italy, but these were meaningless because they "did not apply to the one product that would have made them effective—oil." [48] When the Italian military performance proved ineffectual, the British and French became deeply concerned that, if Mussolini were denied a conquest in Ethiopia, he might seek revenge in Central Europe or against the sponsors of the League sanctions. Thus, on December 8, Sir Samuel Hoare, the British Foreign Secretary, made a deal with French Premier Laval in which the two countries acquiesced in the acquisition by Italy of the major portion of Ethiopia. News of the deal leaked out and caused a major wave of indignation and protest in Britain, forcing Hoare to resign. The British were still determined not to risk war, and they successfully resisted the imposition of oil sanctions by the League. It was not until March 1936 that the Italian campaign in Ethiopia began to achieve success, and the brave resistance of the small African nation was finally broken in May.[49]

The turning point in this period came on March 7, 1936, when Hitler occupied the Rhineland. The Rhineland, which lay between France and Germany and had been demilitarized under provisions of Versailles and Locarno, had been the very foundation of the French strategic position in Europe. "Remilitarization of the Rhineland," as Ulam has succinctly written, "thus at one stroke abolished France's ascendancy on the Continent and deprived her of the possibility of pursuing an independent foreign policy." [50] In the League, Litvinov shrewdly analyzed the meaning of Hitler's action and stated that the Soviet government "is ready to take part in all measures that

48. Fontaine, p. 88.
49. Carr, pp. 226–28; Churchill, chap. 10; Margaret George, *The Warped Vision* (Pittsburgh, Pa.: University of Pittsburgh Press, 1965), chap. 5: A. J. P. Taylor, *The Origins of the Second World War* (New York: Atheneum, 1966), pp. 94–95.
50. Ulam, p. 234.

may be proposed to the Council of the League. . . ."[51] Whether Stalin was genuine in this offer cannot be known, because the French government, fearful of authorizing a mobilization with general elections forthcoming and faced with the British determination to avoid war, decided not to oppose Hitler's action.[52] From the moment of her acquiescence in the militarization of the Rhineland, France's foreign policy was subordinated to British control, and her agreements of mutual assistance with Czechoslovakia and Russia became virtually meaningless. Her only hope for defense in Eastern Europe lay in her pact with Russia, but for Stalin the value of the Franco-Russian treaty of 1935 was seriously, if not fatally, undercut. Now Germany could fortify her Western frontier, and this meant the one thing that the Soviet leaders feared the most—the eastward expansion of Germany.

The Spanish Civil War, which erupted in July 1936 when Franco's rightists revolted against Spain's democratic Popular Front Government, is one of the more interesting and intricate chapters of the painful history of this time. The struggle in Spain formed the pretext for the union of Germany, Japan, and later Italy into an "Anti-Comintern" pact. The war itself provided little in the way of tangible gains for Hitler or Mussolini, but it was almost a miniature preview of the future. Spain provided a testing ground for many of Germany's new weapons, and as such it was a striking illustration of the horror and brutality of Nazi tactics, such as in the bombing of civilians at Guernica. It showed, as in the case of Ethiopia, that Britain would not risk war to halt fascist aggression; this case was particularly tragic because the League policy of "nonintervention", pushed through at British insistence, actually prevented the legitimate government of Spain from receiving desperately needed military supplies while the rightist rebels were well supplied by open and unopposed German-Italian intervention. Furthermore, the Spanish War gave Stalin what was probably his first real

51. Fleming, p. 60.
52. Ulam, p. 235.

dilemma in dealing with the volatile anti-Bolshevik prejudices of the West.

When Stalin sought cooperation with the West to curb Hitler, he "tried to disarm the suspicions, the fears, and the prejudices of the West by moderation and pliability. He tried to lay the ghosts of the past, the giant ghost of world revolution first of all." [53] The dramatic change in the Comintern line in 1935 was clearly a diplomatic gesture to the West. But Stalin could not win on this point, as Issac Deutscher explains:

No matter how moderate and "purely" democratic, how constitutional and "purely" patriotic, were the slogans he had composed for the Popular Fronts, he could not undo the revolutionary potentialities of those "Fronts." Willy-nilly, he had to develop those potentialities and use them to his advantage. The electoral victories of the Popular Front in France and Spain almost automatically raised the anticapitalist temper and the confidence of the working classes. . . . The French and Spanish Communist leaders could not disassociate themselves from that mood of the masses. France was shaken by strikes, mass meetings, and demonstrations of unseen power. Spain was in the throes of civil war. The whole of Western Europe was laboring under new social strains and stresses. Though the Communist leaders, pressed by Moscow, often did their best to put brakes upon the movement, events struck fear into. the hearts of the middle classes, stirring latent sympathy for fascism and fanning distrust of Russia. Thus, by a curious dialectical process, the Popular Fronts defeated their own purpose. They had set out to reconcile the bourgeois west with Russia; but as the strength of their pressure grew, it widened the gulf between the would-be allies. In the eyes of the French and British upper classes Litvinov's calls for collective security and appeals to British and French self-interest became associated with the sit-down strikes, the forty-hour week, the high wages, and the other social reforms which the Popular Front wrested from France's stagnant economy.[54]

53. Deutscher, p. 422.
54. Ibid., p. 423.

The Spanish Civil War presented Stalin with a dilemma that really had no acceptable solution. It was in Stalin's interest to see Franco defeated, both because he had openly committed himself to an anti-Fascist policy and because the already bad French strategic position would have further deteriorated as a result of having a fascist regime on both of her continental fronts.[55] For the first several months of the war, Stalin strictly adhered to a policy of nonintervention. But as the struggle in Spain rapidly became a rallying point for liberals and progressives throughout the world, Russian nonintervention became "clearly inconceivable" for Stalin.[56] "Yet," as Ulam points out, "the complete identification of communism with the cause of Spain was almost as undesirable as a victory of fascism." Finally, in October 1936, Stalin intervened in Spain with military advisers, munitions, and medical supplies, although he would not commit troops as the Germans and Italians had openly done. He went to pains to assure that his interventions would not be associated with the communist cause, but committed a familiar excess in his purge of the more radical and anarchist elements of the Spanish Left. According to Fontaine,

> The "Red" excesses—in particular the profaning of churches and cemeteries, which were helpfully reported by a press that was more discreet when it came to the atrocities of the other side—had awakened a shudder of horror in France and England, comparable to that which stirred public opinion in the West after the Russian Revolution.[57]

Deutscher elaborates:

> The prime motive behind all these doings was Stalin's desire to preserve for the Spanish Popular Front its republican respectability and to avoid antagonizing the British and the French governments. He saved nobody's respectability and he antagonized everybody. Conservative opinion in the

55. Ibid.
56. Ulam, p. 244.
57. Fontaine, p. 89.

West, not interested in the internecine struggle of the Spanish left and confused by the intricacies of Stalin's policy, blamed Stalin as the chief fomenter of revolution.[58]

That Stalin's heavy-handedness and authoritarian excesses alienated public opinion in the West and made alliance with Britain and France more difficult is beyond question. However, without intending or desiring to wash any blood from Stalin's hands, I must judge the impact of his brutal ways in context. Stalin was not the only brutal dictator on the scene at that time. England and France would have to come to terms with Hitler or Stalin. If the practice of frightful atrocities were the sole criterion by which the most preferable dictator were chosen, there is little doubt who would have been most repugnant to Britain. Yet it was Hitler whom Britain courted. These were bloody, ruthless days, and if Hitler's excesses were not too much for the British leaders to swallow when they pursued appeasement, then Stalin's excesses could also have been stomached *had Baldwin or Chamberlain desired coöperation with Russia against Hitler*. Sir Edward Halifax, a principal architect of Chamberlain's anti-Soviet policy, had often criticized Anthony Eden, his predecessor as Foreign Secretary, as being "too strong" in his revulsion from dictators, since "you have got to live with the devils whether you like them, or not." [59] It was not beyond the capabilities of the intelligence-gathering apparatus of a major power to see that Stalin's purge in Spain, however unpalatable, was meant as an expression of his conservatism with respect to world revolution; it was a signal that Stalin could be counted on to control foreign communists and protect Republican governments. Whether or not the British discerned the obvious in Stalin's actions is irrelevant; the essential observation is that they did not *want* to see the meaning of what Stalin did because they had no desire or intention to come to terms with the Soviet Union.

58. Deutscher, p. 425.
59. Frederick Winston Birkenhead, *Halifax: the Life of Lord Halifax* (London: Hamish Hamilton Ltd., 1965), pp. 379–80.

2

The Seeds Are Planted

In the previous chapter I attempted to describe and analyze, in the context of the development of the Cold War, the events from the consolidation of Bolshevik power in Russia (1921) to roughly the end of Stanley Baldwin's term as Prime Minister of England (1937). Considerably more attention was directed toward Soviet foreign policy for the simple reason that, in terms of East-West contacts, it was the Soviet Union that made virtually all the initiatives; it was Russia, not the capitalist nations of the West, particularly England and France, whose strategic and diplomatic position was weak and uncertain. The West really desired no serious political cooperation with Russia at this time, with the possible exception of France who, sharing her Western border with Germany, had an interest in preserving her treaty with Moscow; there is certainly no evidence that a military alliance with Russia was seriously considered in the West, and France, whose alliance with Moscow included nominal military commitments, refused to enter into staff talks that might have given any meaning to the military agreement. Unlike Stalin, the Western leaders prior to 1937 really had no well-defined or systematic policy toward Germany or Italy. The actions of the British and French governments are those of leaders paralyzed by weakness, fear, and misunderstanding: weakness as a result of their failure to respond to Germany's rearming; fear of war; and a misunderstanding of both Hitler and Stalin. This fundamental misunderstanding of the dictators was perhaps excusable in the case of Hitler up to his seizure of the Rhineland in 1936, but much harder to justify or comprehend in the case of Stalin, except from the perspective that a deep aversion to Bolshevism and a virtual paranoia that tended to associate most social reform with communism so blinded the ruling elites (if I may use that term loosely) in the West that they could not rationally analyze the policy of the Soviet Union.

Stanley Baldwin failed to lead British foreign policy, with the result that there was no consistent policy based on systematic assumptions and goals. E. H. Carr has described the conflicting trends in British foreign policy up to the first half of 1935:

> During the first two years after the Nazi revolution, British opinion as a whole was too deeply moved by Nazi excesses to feel much sympathy for German grievance and aspirations; and the British government, though unwilling itself to undertake any commitments, had encouraged the French, the Italian and the Soviet governments to build up a system of defensive alliances for the maintenance of the status quo, particularly in Central Europe where it seemed most directly menaced. But by January 1935, when this system of alliances had been virtually completed by the Franco-Italian reconciliation [brought about by the alienation of Italy from Germany in the winter of 1933–34] indignation in Great Britain against the Nazi regime began to subside. A growing body of opinion came around to the view that the only effect of the French understanding with Italy and the Soviet Union was to isolate and encircle Germany and to perpetuate the inequalities of the Versailles Treaty—in short, to maintain those very con-

ditions which had been largely responsible for the Nazi revolution. Those who held this opinion, while not denying that Germany might be a danger to peace, believed that French, Italian and Soviet policy merely aggravated that danger, and that the British government's first aim should be to break the ring round Germany, to engage in friendly discussions of her grievances, and to bring her back to the League of Nations. [Foreign Secretary] Simon's visit to Berlin [in March 1935] was a concession to this trend of thought.[1]

It was this latter trend, commonly known as appeasement, that gained the upper hand by the end of 1935. Although Britain had supported sanctions against Italy in the fall of 1935, her paramount desire was to avoid war, and by December, fearful of Italian reaction in the face of the lack of success of the aggression in Ethiopia, Britain was willing to hand over most of the African colony to Italy. When this failed because of the public outrage in England, Italy proceeded with her military campaign, which triumphed in May 1936. In July of that year Britain sponsored a move in the League to remove sanctions from Italy. The Anglo-German Naval agreement, as well as Britain's acquiescence in the militarization of the Rhineland and the German-Italian intervention in the Spanish Civil War, clearly indicated the policy preferred by the British Cabinet.

A year before he succeeded Baldwin as Prime Minister, Chamberlain, then Chancellor of the Exchequer, complained in his diary that "we have no policy." On April 27, 1936, he wrote that the failure of the League to protect Ethiopia "demonstrated the failure of collective security." He explained his conception of the proper foreign policy for maintaining peace:

for peace we should depend on a system of regional pacts, to be registered and approved by the League. . . . I thought the proposal would make it easier for Germany to come into the League, and I was anxious that Halifax should visit Berlin and get into touch with Hitler as soon as possible.[2]

1. Carr, pp. 220–21.
2. Keith Feiling, *The Life of Neville Chamberlain* (London: MacMillan and Co., 1947), pp. 295–96.

On June 10, in a speech before the 1900 Club, Chamberlain argued for a policy based on the assumption that "nations cannot be relied upon" to go to war "unless their vital interests are threatened." "That being so," he continued, "does it not suggest that it might be wise to explore the possibilities of localizing the danger spots of the world . . . by means of regional arrangements . . . which should be guaranteed only by those nations whose interests were vitally connected with those danger zones?" [3]

The thrust of the policy Chamberlain wished to pursue as of the spring of 1936 was made apparent by the above-quoted passages. He saw the best guarantee for peace in "regional pacts" to "localize" areas of potential danger not vitally connected with Great Britain. By such a policy he would hope to draw Germany back into cooperation with England. As of early 1936 Chamberlain advocated a rearmament program based on the theory that in the "next war" air power would be of decisive importance with sea power secondary and regular territorial armies of the least value in defense.[4] He embraced this theory not for its value as a realistic contingency in the event of a continental war but rather as a deterrent to the outbreak of war, enabling British diplomacy to follow the line he advocated. On February 9, 1936, he wrote in his diary: "I am pretty satisfied now that, if we can keep out of war for a few years, we shall have an air force of such striking power that no one will care to run risks with it." [5] In another diary entry, upon his assuming the post of Prime Minister, he wrote: "I believe the double policy of rearmament and better relations with Germany and Italy will carry us safely through the danger period, if only the Foreign Office will play up." [6]

Chamberlain's "double policy" was doomed from lack of realism in each of its elements. I have already mentioned the

3. Ibid., p. 296.
4. Ibid., chap. 22.
5. Ibid., pp. 313–14.
6. Ibid., p. 319.

lack of realism with regard to Hitler, but I am willing to admit that even as of March 1938 it *was* conceivable that England, through massive concessions, might have come to terms with Hitler and avoided war. But Chamberlain doomed this remote chance, on which his entire policy was based, by striving for a defense program that let Germany (and all other countries) know that Britain was not prepared for and thus did not intend to fight in a war on the European Continent. It is inconceivable that Hitler could have studied British rearmament, in which the size of the army was severely limited, and not have known that England had no intention of fighting on the Continent. This alone put virtually all the diplomatic cards in Hitler's hand; it made Hitler a negotiating partner who knew that the other side had almost no means of resisting his demands. Chamberlain's frank statement that his projected policy "will carry us safely through the danger period," taken in the context of his intention to strengthen *only* the air force to the extent "that no one will care to run risks with it" makes it clear that he did not seriously anticipate a war.[7] He was aware of the dangers of war, but he was confident that by appeasement he could at least postpone war until his rearmament plans were fulfilled, at which time the very presence of Britain's awesome air force would deter war in Europe.

Chamberlain understood that in the fateful period during which British rearmament was carried out he would have to make particularly attractive offers and perhaps otherwise unconscionable concessions to Germany and Italy to assure their cooperation with England. Despite mutual French-British commitments, Chamberlain had no confidence in France as a strong ally: "France's weakness is a public danger," he wrote in the first month of 1938.[8] Hiding behind the broad mantle of "the English people," he described Britain's position as "one of great anxiety" pending rearmament. Thus, "in the absence of any powerful ally, and until our armaments are completed, we must

7. See also Churchill, pp. 242, 333–34.
8. Feiling, p. 322.

adjust our foreign policy to our circumstances, and even bear
with patience and good humor actions which we should like to
treat in a very different fashion." [9]

It was true, as Chamberlain stated, that Britain lacked a
powerful ally who might have made a different policy toward
Germany feasible; it was not true, however, that Britain could
not have had such an ally if she so desired. The Soviet Union had
repeatedly offered an alliance to Britain and France, and Britain
would not hear of it. The most significant Soviet offers com-
menced in March 1938 when Hitler invaded Austria. Chamberlain, for the next year, gave no serious thought to such an
alliance and only in April 1939 did he even make the pretense
of considering it. What were the reasons for Chamberlain's
negative policy toward Russia? This is perhaps the most crucial
historical question of the pre-World War II period. In this and
the next chapter I will present my answer to this question.

Briefly stated, if not perhaps oversimplified, Chamberlain
rebuffed Stalin's overtures for alliance for two reasons: (1) His
policy was to settle Britain's differences with Hitler, and an
alliance with Russia would have been the antithesis of this
policy; and (2) he was absolutely unwilling to permit what an
alliance with Russia would have entailed, namely, a foothold for
the Soviet Union in Europe and diplomatic relations on an
equal basis as a "great power." It is this thesis that I will substantiate in this and the following chapter.

The most effective way to present my analysis of the com-
plicated and often misunderstood period from 1937 to 1939 is
chronologically. One factor vital to understanding British policy
in context must be addressed, however, before the chronological
analysis is attempted. One of the common contemporary as well
as historical justifications for disregarding Russia as a potential
ally is that Stalin's 1937–38 army purges had so undermined
the strength and effectiveness of the Russian Army that it could
not be counted on in the offensive capacity that an alliance

9. Ibid., pp. 323–24.

would have demanded. A. J. P. Taylor's analysis of this justification is probably the best:

> The British and French governments acknowledged Soviet Russia (in 1938) only to emphasize her military weakness; and this view, though it rested no doubt on their information, represented also their desire. They wanted Soviet Russia to be excluded from Europe; and therefore readily assumed that she was so by circumstances.[10]

That Britain and France believed in the ineffectiveness of the Soviet Army because that belief best served their policy toward Germany and Eastern Europe is undoubtedly true; that this belief rested on the intelligence they were receiving is not completely true.

The British military attaché in Moscow, Colonel Firebrace, wrote an evaluation of the Soviet Army on April 18, 1938. He emphasized the drastic effects of the purges on the Army's leadership and concluded that militarily "there must be considerable doubt as to whether the Soviet Union is capable of" a war of offense; "In defense of its territory, I still consider that the Red Army would be a formidable opponent."[11] In a conversation with French Premier Daladier on April 29, British Foreign Minister Halifax included the effects of the purges as one of the factors that "made it extremely doubtful whether Russia could be counted upon to make any great contribution, if, indeed, she could make any contribution at all" to the defense of Czechoslovakia. Daladier agreed that the purge had weakened the Red Army. He pointed out, however, that numerically the Soviet Air Force was the "strongest" in Europe and that Russia's "potential war resources were extremely great."[12] On July 26 French Foreign Minister Bonnet told U.S. Ambassador William Bullitt and U.S. Treasury Secretary Morganthau that he "believed that the recent 'purges' . . . had so weakened the . . . Red Army and

10. Taylor, p. 163.
11. DBFP, 1: 162–65.
12. Ibid., pp. 213, 218.

the government that it would be impossible for the Soviet Union to contemplate war beyond its frontiers." [13] Yet, in a conversation with Halifax in September, Daladier again drew attention to Russia's air supremacy.[14]

The above estimates relate to the possibility of Soviet military assistance, in compliance with her treaty obligations, in the event of aggression against Czechoslovakia. According to the 1935 treaty with Prague, Russia could act only if France chose to act first. Of course, in 1938 France was not about to go to war over Czechoslovakia. During this period the Soviet government repeatedly gave its assurances that it was willing to fulfill its treaty obligations if (1) France acted first and (2) France arranged for the passage of Soviet troops across Poland or Rumania; these stipulations were entirely justified and, in fact, necessary. Without them, there was no possibility that Soviet military aid could be rendered. France, of course, had an interest in keeping alive the alternative of securing Russia's help in the event of war, if only because of her own treaty with Prague. But Britain was firmly committed not to precipitate war over Czechoslovakia; hence it was actually in the interest of her policy that Russia *not* intervene. It is important to remember that, by this time, France could not pursue an independent foreign policy; she had to bow to Britain's wishes. It was for these reasons, I believe, that the British evidenced such skepticism about the prospects of *any* Soviet military aid, whereas Daladier apparently regarded the Soviet Air Force as a probable asset in the event of war over Czechoslovakia.

In this context it is extremely interesting to note a conversation of May 15, 1938, in Moscow between British chargé Vereker and French Ambassador Coulondre. Coulondre had requested the meeting because he anticipated a request from his government for information regarding possible Russian reactions to a

13. U.S. Department of State, *Foreign Relations of the United States: 1938* (Washington, D.C.: Government Printing Office), 1: 58. (Hereinafter referred to as FRUS.)
14. DBFP, 2: 533.

German attack on Czechoslovakia. He had got the impression from Litvinov that Russia was becoming "more serious in regard to" the possibility of taking action in Czechoslovakia. In sounding out Vereker, Coulondre summarized his most recent intelligence:

> We knew . . . that the army on the whole was more con-tented than it had ever been and was certainly better fed than the whole of the remaining population, that they had enormous supplies of ammunition, some thousands of tanks, and quite a formidable, if obsolescent, air force, and that he had moreover been reliably informed that M. Voroshilov had reported to M. Stalin that the Soviet army was fit for war and that he had also heard from his Bulgarian colleague that, in order to forestall any possible revolt on the part of the peasants in the event of mobilization, a large number of able-bodied conscripts had in fact already been attached to units to increase their peacetime strength.
>
> Another factor which he considered should not be omitted from our calculations in estimating the Russian situation was the military situation in the Far East. . . . [recent develop-ments] had undoubtedly led the Kremlin into thinking that any possible Japanese menace to their interests in the Far East had for the present been deflected down into Central China, thus relieving the Soviet government of much anxiety on that score and enabling them thereby to make if necessary a correspondingly greater effort in the West. M. Coulondre therefore felt that one could in fact place some reliance on the Soviet government both in a political and in a military sense at the present juncture, and that on the whole he felt inclined to tell the Quai d'Orsay that he was more optimistic of possible Russian intervention on the side of Czechoslovakia at the present moment than he had been heretofore.[15]

Vereker disagreed with Coulondre, and Colonel Fireside was present to discuss in detail the effect of the purges on the Red Army's high command. The discussion was informal, but Vereker tried to discourage any "vain hopes" on the part of the French Ambassador of the value or reliability of Russian aid "as a counterpoise to the Germans." [16]

15. Ibid., 1: 305.
16. Ibid., pp. 306–7.

Coulondre's intelligence, if accurate, would seem to detract from the validity of the British interpretation of Soviet military effectiveness. His emphasis on the Soviet position in the Far East was well founded. In 1937, the threat of a Japanese attack was far more imminent than that of a German attack.[17] Faced with threatening border clashes, the primary Soviet interest in the first half of 1937 was to have China absorb Japan's fury; following Japan's invasion of China on July 7, 1937, "the Kremlin could breathe more freely." Adam Ulam has confirmed Coulondre's contemporaneous analysis: "By 1938 the situation in the Far East still required the utmost watchfulness, but the danger of war . . . had passed. Europe once more occupied the main stage." [18]

This situation was soon to change, however. In July 1938 serious fighting erupted between Russian and Japanese forces at the border area of Changkufeng, involving "tens of thousands of troops, planes, and artillery." [19] By August, the Russians had repulsed the Japanese. Ulam writes that "the Russian's spirited action must have given the Japanese general staff some second thoughts about the allegedly debilitating effect of the purges on the Soviet military establishment." [20] Evidently the British were unimpressed by this demonstration. On March 26, 1939, Chamberlain wrote in his diary, "I have no confidence whatever in [Russia's] ability to maintain an effective offensive, even if she wanted to." [21] Halifax expressed similar sentiments on March 24.[22] From May until August 1939 Soviet forces were involved in massive battles with the Japanese along the Mongolian frontier. They again repulsed the Japanese and gave an "impressive performance." [23]

It was in April 1939 that Britain began guaranteeing states

17. Ulam, p. 248.
18. Ibid., p. 250.
19. Ibid., p. 254.
20. Ibid.
21. Feiling, p. 403.
22. *New York Times Magazine,* July 18, 1943.
23. Rubinstein, pp. 114–15.

in Eastern Europe, where she was clearly powerless to act "except," Churchill notes, "within the framework of a general agreement with Russia." [24] Now Britain was willing to negotiate with Russia, but only on the basis that Russia commit herself to give unilateral aid subject to Poland's and Rumania's approval. The notion was preposterous and, as I will discuss in detail later, Britain participated in the negotiations less because she desired Soviet military aid than because she hoped the prospect of a pact with Russia would give her a diplomatic advantage in coming to terms with Hitler. As I will later document, Chamberlain based this policy, in part, on the assumption that Poland and Rumania together could defend themselves with minimal British and French aid in the event of a German invasion. Yet, on April 5, 1939, the British Ambassador in Warsaw had provided a wealth of intelligence information proving that the state of Polish defense was not adequate to resist invasion. "The importance for Poland of a friendly Russia is thus of paramount importance," he wrote. Along with the military intelligence he included in his report to the Foreign Office were these two essential factors: (1) "The attitude of the U.S.S.R. is vital to Poland from the point of view of supplies for her armed forces"; and (2) "the Polish air force equipment is . . . inadequate [to resist German invasion] but it is probably no less inadequate than the equipment of much in the rest of Poland's armed forces." [25]

The sincerity of the whole British attitude toward Soviet military effectiveness is brought into question by all of these facts. To say the least, the British were selective in accepting or even seeking intelligence on which to base an estimate of Russian capabilities as of the middle of 1938. Regardless of their skepticism at the time of the crisis over Czechoslovakia, the British, it must be noted, never took the Russians up on their repeated calls for joint action or their pledges to fulfill their treaty obligations. If the British genuinely doubted the ability of the Red

24. Churchill, p. 362.
25. DBFP, 5: 38–44.

Army but nevertheless contemplated the possibility of standing up to Hitler, they would still have had to make an effort to consult directly with the Russians on matters about which they were currently only able to speculate on the basis of information they freely admitted was uncertain and unreliable; this they never did. Furthermore, whatever their feelings about the Red Army, the British had no way to make good on their pledges of 1939 to Poland or Rumania without Russia's aid, and this they did not really want until it was too late to secure it. In short, the most that can be said about Britain's analysis and conclusions of Soviet military effectiveness in the 1938–39 period is that the British leaders operated in a political, not objective or factual context. Furthermore, the military advice and evaluations offered by the British Chiefs of Staff were significantly influenced by diplomatic considerations. In February 1938, the Chiefs resisted pressure for staff talks with French and Belgian military delegations. Such talks were a necessary prerequisite to any cooperative defense plans that the three nations might make in fulfillment of their mutual treaty obligations. Yet, as Anthony Eden relates :

> In our present effort to reach a detente with Germany, the Chiefs of Staff argued that it was most important, from the military standpoint, that we should not appear to have both feet in the French camp. They therefore considered that the military plans for closer collaboration with the French upon concerted measures against Germany, however logical they might appear, would be outweighed by the grave risk of precipitating the very situation we wished to avoid, namely, the irreconcilable suspicion and hostility of Germany.[26]

Eden's secretary, Oliver Harvey, was more blunt in his personal diary. Of the Chiefs of Staff he wrote: "They are terrified of any cooperation with the French." [27] If the Chiefs feared alienating Germany by consulting with England's ally, one can

26. Eden, pp. 566–67.
27. John Harvey, *The Diplomatic Diaries of Oliver Harvey, 1937–40* (New York: St. Martin's Press, 1970), p. 89.

imagine their attitude toward the very thought of an alliance with the country which Hitler openly called his foremost enemy, the Soviet Union. It is therefore not unreasonable to question the integrity and impartiality of the evaluations of Russia's military capacity that the Chiefs of Staff provided for the Chamberlain Cabinet. The Chiefs themselves in the spring of 1939 were to reverse their position on the value of Russia as a military ally, a reversal in which they freely admitted that "strategical and political aspects are closely related." [28] Ironically, when Colonel Firebrace wrote his evaluation of the Red Army, he had to account for the difference in other countries' estimates of Russia's capability to wage war in the near future. Why should other nations be more optimistic than his? He wrote, "in general their opinions are to some extent swayed by their desires." [29]

Admittedly, this discussion has taken place out of context. One may criticize the British for their apparent unwillingness to seriously evaluate all military factors relating to Russia's possible participation in an alliance guaranteeing East Europe; but this is, in fact, incidental. Whether or not the British really believed what they said about Soviet military effectiveness, and however questionable the validity or realism of their analysis, that belief was *not* the reason that Britain rejected an alliance with Russia.

Chamberlain, Halifax, Wilson, Hoare, and Henderson (and many others involved in making British policy) all had a fundamental hatred of Bolshevism and a profound distrust of Russia. Under Secretary of State Alexander Cadogan wrote in his diary in 1938 that Chamberlain had "what amounted to a hatred of the Russians," adding that "we have all come to loathe (them)."[30] To the men who made British foreign policy, an alliance with the Soviet Union recognizing Russian interests in Eastern Europe and paving the way for the penetration of Bolshevism into that

28. Ian Colvin, *The Chamberlain Cabinet* (London: Victor Gollancz Ltd., 1971), pp. 211–12.

29. DBFP, 1: 164.

30. David Dilks, *The Diaries of Sir Alexander Cadogan, 1938–1945* (New York: G. P. Putnam's Sons, 1972), p. 53.

area was unthinkable. "A thoroughness of commitment to Russia," writes one historian of the period, ". . . would have been anathema to those in power" in Britain.[31] Describing the flip attitude of the British Cabinet toward the 1939 negotiations with Moscow, another prominent analyst writes: "Behind it all was a deep, insuperable aversion to Bolshevist (*sic*) Russia." [32] In June 1939 William Bullitt spoke with French Foreign Minister Bonnet about the lack of progress in the negotiations with Moscow; Bonnet reflected the attitude of the Chamberlain Government when he said that "France and England could certainly not consent to giving the Soviet Union support for an extension of Bolshevism in Eastern Europe." [33] Yet up to that time the whole policy of France and England had been based on supporting and facilitating the extension of Nazi Germany into Central Europe.

Chamberlain's distrust of Russia exceeded .the bounds of reason. On March 20, 1938, after the Russians had called for joint action to guarantee Czechoslovakia, he wrote that "the Russians [are] stealthily and cunningly pulling all the strings behind the scenes to get us involved in a war with Germany." [34] Indeed, to a man who believed this, what difference did Russia's offensive military capacity make? A year later, when he was coming around to the realization that some accord with Russia would be necessary if a stand against Nazi aggression was to be taken, Chamberlain still could write: "I must confess the most profound distrust of Russia. . . . And I distrust her motives, which seem to me to have little connection with our ideas of liberty, and to be concerned only with getting everyone else by the ears." [35]

Nazi Germany certainly had "little connection" with British

31. Christopher Thorne, *The Approach of War, 1938–39* (New York: St. Martin's Press, 1967), p. 140.
32. L. B. Namier, *Diplomatic Prelude, 1938–39* (London: MacMillan and Co., 1948), p. 188.
33. FRUS (1939), 1: 266–69.
34. Feiling, p. 347.
35. Ibid., p. 403.

"ideas of liberty," and Chamberlain could privately admit to a profound distrust of Hitler. Why, then, did Chamberlain try to accommodate Hitler? First, the price of opposing Hitler was considered too high to pay. Chamberlain wanted to avoid war, especially war over Central or Eastern Europe, an area not vital to British interests and in which the British would need the help of Soviet Russia to wage war. He believed that he could pacify Hitler, or at least protect Western Europe, by granting Hitler hegemony in Central Europe. Also, there can be little doubt, as Halifax, Henderson, and Wilson freely admitted to Hitler, that a strong and anti-Bolshevik Germany was regarded as a benefit and protection for Europe, provided she would cooperate peacefully with the capitalist nations. Economically, Chamberlain was always conscious of the fact that Germany was "a rising market." [36]

It is fundamental to any understanding of appeasement to point out that this policy was *not* forced on the Chamberlain Cabinet because Britain was militarily unprepared to pursue any other policy; rather, as of the end of Chamberlain's first year as Prime Minister, the vulnerable state of British defenses was the result of a series of deliberate policy decisions based on a strong faith in the rightness and practicality of appeasement. Chamberlain was confident that he could circumvent the need for massive rearmament by altering the European status quo in a manner acceptable to Hitler.

When Chamberlain assumed office in 1937, Britain was hardly capable of defending herself militarily, was unable to fulfill her continental commitments, and did not possess the capacity to produce the armaments necessary to expand her military machine. This situation was directly the result of the irresponsible maneuverings of Stanley Baldwin, who had manipulated the issue of rearmament, as he had so many other issues, as a tool for his own political advancement, not as a matter of vital interest for his country.

In Parliament on February 7, 1934, Winston Churchill made

36. Ibid., p. 329.

a plea for the expansion of British air power in the face of an expansion-minded and rearming Germany; should "the means of threatening the heart of the British Empire pass into the hands of the present rulers of Germany," England would lose her "freedom of action and independence." Prime Minister Baldwin responded with the pledge that

> if all our efforts for [a disarmament] agreement fail . . . then any Government of this country—a National Government more than any, and *this* Government—will see to it that in air strength and air power this country shall no longer be in a position inferior to any country within striking distance of its shores.[37]

When Churchill and some of his colleagues declared in Commons on November 28, 1934, that British military preparations were insufficient and that by 1937 the Germans would possess superior air power, Baldwin responded that the projections of the Air Ministry belied Churchill's arguments, and that Churchill's figures are considerably exaggerated." [38] Baldwin's lack of foresight was striking. By May 22 of the following year he was forced to admit that his estimates for the future were "completely wrong. We were completely misled on that subject." [39] In the general election of October 1935, Baldwin played both sides of the fence on the rearmament issue, pleasing those who favored sanctions against Italy by speaking "in strong terms of the need for rearmament," and then, "very anxious to comfort the professional peace-loving elements in the nation," declaring to the Peace Society "I give you my word there will be no great armaments." [40] By the end of 1936 Britain was seriously behind Germany in air power, and Churchill "severely reproached" Baldwin for failing to keep his pledge that Britain would never become inferior in air power to any nation within striking distance. This

37. Churchill, pp. 112–13.
38. Ibid., pp. 118–19.
39. Ibid., p. 123.
40. Ibid., pp. 179–80.

prompted Baldwin's famous speech of November 12, 1936, in which he "carried naked truth about his motives into indecency" by hiding behind a pacifist sentiment that he probably more than any other politician had helped create by misinforming his people about German rearmament:

> Supposing I had gone to the country and said that Germany was rearming, and we must rearm, does anybody think that this pacific democracy would have rallied to that cry at that moment? I cannot think of anything that would have made the loss of the election from my point of view more certain.[41]

Churchill was right when he wrote that "the passionate desire for peace which animated the uninformed, misinformed majority of the British people . . . is no excuse for political leaders who fall short of their duty." [42]

Chamberlain too opposed any full-scale rearmament, for a wide variety of reasons. At the heart of his opposition seems to have been an unwillingness or inability to recognize the militant ambitions of Hitler and the untenable diplomatic position into which Britain would be forced vis-à-vis Germany if she did not keep pace with the latter's rearmament. Chamberlain and his supporters feared the economic consequences of putting the country on a war production basis, and they reasoned, in the face of significant if small opposition, that the international situation simply did not warrant such a commitment on Britain's part. At the end of 1936 Halifax expressed this general sentiment in response to a call by Churchill for the establishment of a Ministry of Supply. Halifax, then in the House of Lords, maintained that the European situation was not sufficiently grave to warrant transforming Britain into an "armed camp":

> What is quite certain is that in the process you would gravely dislocate trade, Budgets, general finance, and the

41. Ibid., pp. 215–16.
42. Ibid., p. 112.

general credit of the country. Are we in fact to judge the question so serious that everything has to give way to the military reconditioning of our Defense Forces? Such a conclusion, in fact, appears to me to rest on premises, not only of the inevitability, but of a degree of certainty as to the early imminence of war, which I am not prepared to accept.[43]

As Chancellor of the Exchequer, Chamberlain was concerned with the economic aspects of Britain's armaments program, and he was exasperated at the lack of a consistent policy defining the role and eventual size of each of the military services. At one of the last meetings of the Baldwin Cabinet, on April 28, 1937, Chamberlain called attention to the constantly rising estimates of military spending and the Cabinet's failure to agree upon a definite policy. According to the Cabinet's minutes, "he warned the Cabinet that we were approaching the time when he would have to propose a fixed limit to which the Services would have to conform." [44] The idea that Britain must adopt an armaments policy that fell within a financial ceiling reflected Chamberlain's concern that full rearmament was economically unacceptable. In reviewing the year 1937 in his diary entry for February 19, 1938, Chamberlain expressed this concern:

Again, our own armament programme continued to grow, and to pile up our financial commitments to a truly alarming extent . . . the annual cost of maintenance, after we had finished rearmament, seemed likely to be more than we could find without heavily increased taxation for an indefinite period.[45]

As Anthony Eden has written in his Memoirs:

A difficulty which confronted the British Government at this period was that a high priority . . . was placed on the maintenance of our economic stability. This argument found particular favour with the Prime Minister and was constantly

43. Birkenhead, pp. 357–58.
44. Colvin, pp. 31–32.
45. Feiling, p. 322.

used by the Treasury, but it certainly made difficulties for the Service departments, whose political chiefs and staffs had to spend many hours trying to curb their demands within Treasury figures which had no particular significance in terms of defense.[46]

In a memorandum of December 1937, Thomas Inskip, Minister for the Coordination of Defense, defended the philosophy that economic strength was in itself a deterrent to war, of more value in fact than bankrupting rearmament:

> The maintenance of credit facilities and our general balance of trade are of vital importance, not merely from the point of view of our strength in peace time, but equally for purposes of war. This country cannot hope to win a war against a major power by a sudden knockout blow: on the contrary, for success we must contemplate a long war. . . . We must therefore confront our enemies with the risks of a long war, which they cannot face. If we are to emerge victoriously from such a war, it is essential that we should enter it with sufficient economic strength to enable us to make the fullest uses of the resources overseas, and to withstand the strain.[47]

The implications of this philosophy were that limitations would have to be placed upon the extent and nature of rearmament and, consequently, the preservation of peace would have to be undertaken almost solely through diplomacy. As Chamberlain wrote in early 1938, "From the first I have been trying to improve relations with the 2 storm centers, Berlin and Rome."[48] Indeed, if Britain were to pursue a policy in which she deliberately deprived herself of the means to resist the demands of Hitler and Mussolini, she would have to bargain (from a position of weakness) to achieve a new status quo in Europe and her colonial empire, one acceptable to the two dictators. When the British Ambassador to Rome warned Sir Robert Vansittart of "the truculent and aggressive attitude of Italy in the

46. Eden, p. 564.
47. Colvin, p. 49.
48. Feiling, p. 322.

Mediterranean," the Cabinet met on July 7, 1937, to consider the issue. Thomas Inskip inquired as to how far this warning should affect Britain's defensive arrangements. Chamberlain, according to the Cabinet minutes, "thought there was very little that could be done to improve matters. The real counter to Italy's disquieting attitude was to get on better terms with Germany." The Cabinet concurred with the Prime Minister's views.[49] By the end of 1937, the view that, in place of full military preparations, diplomacy would have to defend British interests had crystallized into a policy acknowledged and approved by each Cabinet member except Foreign Secretary Anthony Eden.

Eden did not particularly object to efforts at improving relations with the Axis powers, but he viewed such diplomatic attempts as futile and humiliating unless backed up by sufficient military power. In a private meeting with Chamberlain on November 8, 1937, Eden expressed his conviction that "rearmament must go faster. . . . Unless it were known that we were rearming effectively, our efforts in international sphere today were useless." As Eden recorded in his diary, "N.C. did not, I think, share my view and clearly had the financial situation much in mind."[50] A week later, a friend of Oliver Harvey spoke with Chamberlain's confident, Horace Wilson, about the Prime Minister's deteriorating relationship with his Foreign Secretary. According to Wilson, Chamberlain denied any personal hostility, but "at the same time P.M. DID think his own policy of using every opportunity of getting together with the dictators was right and that he was determined to go on with it. P.M. genuinely thought A.E. [Eden] was wrong. . . ."[51]

During November 1937 the British Chiefs of Staff completed a secret memorandum entitled, "A Comparison of the Strength of Great Britain With That of Certain Other Nations As At January 1938." The outlook expressed in this report was bleak, especially in its judgment that France and Russia, the only two

49. Colvin, p. 45.
50. Eden, p. 557.
51. Harvey, p. 61.

major nations with whom Britain could ally in the event of war with Germany, Italy, or Japan, were not sufficiently militarily prepared to be depended on should war erupt. The report's conclusion was highly political, and provided a strong reinforcement for the sentiments already expressed by Chamberlain and his supporters:

> From the above report it will be seen that our Naval, Military and Air Forces, in their present stage of development, are still far from sufficient to meet our defensive commitments, which now extend from Western Europe through the Mediterranean to the Far East. . . . So far as Germany is concerned, as our preparations develop, our defense forces will provide a considerable deterrent to aggression. But the outstanding feature of the present situation is the increasing probability that a war started on any one of these three areas may extend to one or both of the other two. Without overlooking the assistance which we should hope to obtain from France, and possibly other allies, we cannot foresee the time when our defense forces will be strong enough to safeguard our territory, trade and vital interests against Germany, Italy and Japan simultaneously. We cannot therefore, exaggerate the importance, from the point of view of Imperial defense, of any political or international action that can be taken to reduce the numbers of our potential enemies and to gain the support of potential allies.[52]

This secret report was discussed on December 2, 1937, at a meeting of the Committee of Imperial Defense, a Cabinet subcommittee. Anthony Eden took issue with the Chiefs of Staff's report. Pointing to the union of Germany, Italy, and Japan in the anti-Comintern pact, Eden suggested that it would "be a mistake to try to detach any one member" of the pact "by offers of support or acquiescence in the fulfillment of their aims." His conclusion: "it might be more in keeping with our honour and dignity to pursue a policy of armed strength." [53] This position met with severe opposition, especially from Chancellor of the

52. Colvin, pp. 63–64.
53. Ibid., pp. 65–66.

Exchequer Simon, who pointed out that "we are in process of spending 1500 millions on our defense. . . . It is clear that we cannot go on spending at this rate forever, and a political adjustment with one or more of our political enemies is absolutely vital." [54] Chamberlain firmly expressed his agreement with the Chiefs of Staff. "To contemplate basing our defensive preparations on the possibility of a war with Italy, Germany and Japan simultaneously was to set ourselves an impossible problem," he said.[55] He repeated the view that he had often expressed, namely, that "Germany was the real key to the question"; relations with Germany would have to be improved. Furthermore, he stated his intention not to repeat Baldwin's pledge to maintain air parity with Germany, for he "did not consider it necessary to have precise equality in every class of aircraft." [56]

The broad issue was put before the full Cabinet on December 22. Halifax made a strong appeal in favor of the Prime Minister's position:

> we are faced with the possibility of three enemies at once. The conclusion which I draw . . . is that this throws an immensely heavy burden on diplomacy and that we ought to make every possible effort to get on good terms with Germany.[57]

The Cabinet voted in support of Chamberlain. They recognized "factors of economic resources and stability as being essential to the strength and fulfillment of the Defense programmes," and approved a set of defense priorities that deprived Britain of an army for a continental role and postponed final decision on a policy for the expansion of the Air Force.[58]

In pursuit of a far-reaching agreement with Hitler, Cham-

54. Ibid., p. 66.
55. Ibid., p. 64.
56. Ibid., p. 69.
57. Ibid., p. 79.
58. Ibid., pp. 80–88; Col. Roderick Macleod, *The Ironside Diaries, 1937–1940* (London: Constable and Co., 1962), pp. 42–43, 46, 48–49.

berlain sent Halifax to Germany, in response to a German initiative, in November 1937. Although Eden was still Foreign Secretary, Chamberlain did not trust him with the delicate task of building the framework of an agreement with Hitler. Eden, whose influence in the making of British Foreign policy had seriously waned, attempted to instruct Halifax in an effort to assure that British interests were not compromised in these unofficial discussions with Hitler. At the end of October, Eden told Halifax to "confine himself to warning comment on Austria and Czechoslovakia" so as "to discourage German intervention in these two states." [59] Later he instructed that "it is essential to avoid giving the impression of our being in pursuit of" Hitler.[60] Halifax ignored both of these instructions.

On November 19, 1937, Halifax met with Hitler and explained the policy of cooperation that his government wished to pursue. The object was "to achieve a better understanding between England and Germany by means of personal talks with the Führer" for "a comprehensive and frank discussion of all questions affecting the two countries" with a view toward "completely" removing the "existing misunderstandings." [61] Halifax told Hitler that "he and other members of the British Government were fully aware that the Führer had not only achieved a great deal inside Germany herself, but that, by destroying Communism in his country, he had barred its road to Western Europe, and that Germany therefore could rightly be regarded

59. Eden, p. 577.
60. Ibid., p. 578.
61. References to this meeting are from Ministry of Foreign Affairs of the USSR, *Documents and Materials Relating to the Eve of the Second World War,* vol. 1, Doc. No. 1. (Hereinafter referred to as "Documents and Materials".) Another translation of the same minutes of the meeting from German Foreign Ministry files is contained in *Documents on German Foreign Policy,* Series D. vol. 1, No. 31, but this translation is less complete. (Hereinafter referred to as DGFP). Halifax's minutes of the meeting, which corroborate the German version, may be found in his memoirs, *Fulness of Days* (London: Collins, 1957) where it is very selectively edited, and in Birkenhead's biography where a more complete version is provided.

as a bulwark of the West against Bolshevism." He assured Hitler that Britain would exercise her influence to see that "the errors of the Versailles dictate . . . be rectified." He solicited Hitler's views on the League and disarmament and added:

> All other questions could be characterized as relating to changes in the European order, changes that sooner or later would probably take place. To these questions belonged Danzig, Austria and Czechoslovakia. England was only interested that any alterations should be effected by peaceful evolution, so as to avoid methods which might cause far-reaching disturbances, which were not desired by either the Führer or by other countries.

This was hardly a "warning" to Hitler. As Eden later implied, it was more a signal that Britain would acquiesce in any changes in the status quo in Eastern Europe that Germany could effect without resorting to war. Eden recalled:

> I wished that Halifax had warned Hitler more strongly against intervention in Central Europe. "Alterations through the course of peaceful evolution" meant one thing to Halifax and probably something quite different to the Führer. Hitler was capable of taking this as giving him freedom to increase subversive Nazi activity in Austria, or to stir up the grievances of the Sudeten Germans.[62]

Eden clearly exaggerated Halifax's naiveté, for Halifax was quite aware of the implications of what he told Hitler, as his own memorandum of the conversation reveals:

> As regards Austria and Czechoslovakia, I formed the impression that Germany believes time to be on her side, in the sense that the strong magnet will sooner or later attract the steel filings lying about within reach of its attraction, *and intends to assist this process as far as possible.*[63]

In the course of his conversation with Halifax, Hitler raised the colonial question, demanding the return of Germany's former

62. Eden, p. 584.
63. Birkenhead, p. 373.

colonies and hinting at deals by which he might gain portions of other colonial empires. He justified his rearmament in terms of the danger of Soviet Russia, clearly implying that Russia's presence prevented a change in Germany's armament policy. Halifax concluded by expressing Chamberlain's wish that this discussion be followed "by further talks on individual questions." "All that was needed," he said, "was that both sides should have one aim in view, namely, the establishment and consolidation of peace in Europe."

Chamberlain was elated at the "great success" of Halifax's visit "because it achieved its object, that of creating an atmosphere in which it is possible to discuss with Germany the practical questions involved in a European settlement." In his diary entry of November 26, 1937, Chamberlain expressed his confidence in Hitler's and Goering's wish not to make war at present. He wrote:

> Of course, they want to dominate Eastern Europe; they want as close a union with Austria as they can get without incorporating her in the Reich, and they want much the same things for the Sudetendeutsche as we did for the Uitlanders in the Transvaal. . . . I don't see why we shouldn't say to Germany, "give us satisfactory assurances that you won't use force to deal with Austrians and Czechoslovakians, and we will give you similar assurances that we won't use force to prevent the changes you want, if you can get them by peaceful means." [64]

Thus, Chamberlain clearly approved of German hegemony in Eastern Europe, secured by "peaceful means," which really included any means short of open warfare.

The first real challenge to Chamberlain's complacency came in mid-February, when Hitler met with Austrian Chancellor Schuschnigg at Berchtesgaden and presented a series of ultimatums threatening Austria's independence. The immediate reaction of Undersecretary Cadogan was typical of the Cabinet in

64. Feiling, p. 333.

general: "I almost wish Germany would swallow Austria and get it over. She is probably going to do so anyhow—anyhow we can't stop her. What's all this fuss about?"[65] Schuschnigg appealed to Britain for help, but the Cabinet knew it was in a position to do nothing to stop Hitler. William Strang, head of the Central Department of the Foreign Office, analyzed the situation and concluded:

> We do not possess the means to prevent Germany from treating Austria and Czechoslovakia as satellite states. . . . neither we nor the French possess the offensive power to prevent Germany from working her will in Central Europe.[66]

Of course, Chamberlain had no intention of opposing Hitler's designs on Austria. He merely wished to see Hitler get his way without war, and now Hitler's actions drove home the point that the British were simply not in a position to stop Hitler if he wanted war. By February 19, the Cabinet had written off Austria. A Foreign Office memorandum of that date stated that "we must assume that Austria is doomed as an independent state."[67]

On March 8, 1938, the British Ambassador in Berlin, Neville Henderson, met with Hitler for further discussions on the "broad outline [of] an attempt at a solution suggested by the British Government."[68] He stressed Britain's willingness to abide by changes in Europe, provided they were effected without resort to war, and he said that "the purpose of the British proposal was to contribute to" a settlement that avoided war. Hitler, who was preparing to take over Austria in a week, spoke in more detail about his wishes in Eastern Europe. Again he raised the specter of an attack by Russia, saying that "German rearmament was made necessary by Russia." He insisted on complete freedom of action in Eastern Europe and, apparently playing on the well-voiced British dread of war, he made it clear that if

65. Dilks, p. 47.
66. Colvin, p. 99.
67. Ibid.
68. Documents and Materials, No. 3.

Britain opposed his designs in the East, she would force him to make war: "if England continued to oppose the German effort to achieve a just and reasonable settlement here, then the moment would come when it would be necessary to fight." Hitler warned Henderson that "if explosions from within were to occur in Austria or Czechoslovakia, Germany would not remain neutral but would act with lightning speed." This was a thinly veiled threat, since Nazi subversion through "fifth columns" in Austria had created a situation where Hitler could, at his whim, trigger violence that would provoke suppression and would thus "justify" his taking action against Austria.[69] Hitler found a sympathetic listener in Henderson when he charged that agreements with "so barbaric a creation as the Soviet Union" were "as good as worthless." He criticized the admission of Russia into Europe through her treaties with France, Czechoslovakia, and Poland, and reminded Henderson that his (Hitler's) long-standing proposals on disarmament "had in mind a union of Europe without Russia."

On March 10, 1938, the new Foreign Minister, Ribbentrop, wrote Hitler from London that a definite and unmistakable trend in British foreign policy had become apparent since the Halifax visit in November 1937: "It looks as if Chamberlain and Halifax want to try to reach a peaceful understanding among the four Great Powers of Europe without the Soviet Union." [70] The same day, Erich Kordt, Ribbentrop's private secretary, spoke with Sir Horace Wilson in London. Wilson was Chamberlain's "principal confidant and agent," in both foreign and economic matters.[71] In discussing a four-power agreement with Kordt, Wilson said, according to Kordt, "Russia ought to be left out entirely at the present time. In his [Wilson's] opinion the system there was bound 'to melt away' some day." [72]

The following day, March 11, Hitler delivered an ultimatum

69. Churchill, pp. 90–92 and chap. 15; Fleming, p. 91.
70. DGFP, 1: 262.
71. Churchill, pp. 241, 298; Feiling, p. 327.
72. DGFP, 1: 272.

to Schuschnigg, who had, in desperation, announced a plebiscite to determine whether Austria should be incorporated into the Reich or remain independent. On March 12, Nazi troops marched into Austria. Chamberlain received the news of the German ultimatum while he and Halifax were dining with Ribbentrop on the 11th. Halifax could not conceal his indignation at this time. However, later that evening, Chamberlain called Ribbentrop to a private meeting at which he asked the Foreign Minister to convey a message to Hitler: "It had always been his desire to clean up German-British relations. He had now made up his mind to realize this aim . . . this was his sincere wish and firm determination." Chamberlain, whose apparent sincerity impressed the cold and skeptical Ribbentrop, concluded by saying that "once we had all got past this unpleasant affair and a reasonable solution had been found, it was to be hoped that we could begin working in earnest toward a German-British understanding." [73]

March 12 was a sad day for Chamberlain, not because the Austrians had lost their independence without even the façade of a plebiscite, but because Hitler had behaved in a way inconsistent with Chamberlain's wishes; he had excluded a "reasonable solution" by resorting to the use of military force.[74] As Chamberlain and Halifax agreed, "what it was necessary to condemn was the method," not the aim.[75] Chamberlain's diary entry for March 13 is very frank:

> It is perfectly evident, surely, now that force is the only argument Germany understands, and that collective security cannot offer any prospect of preventing such events, until it can show a visible force of overwhelming strength, backed by determination to use it. And if that is so, is it not obvious that such force and determination are most effectively mobilized by alliances, which don't require meetings at Geneva, and resolutions by dozens of small nations who have no

73. Ibid., pp. 276–77.
74. H. H. E. Craster, *Speeches on Foreign Policy by Viscount Halifax* (London: Oxford University Press, 1940), p. 125. (Hereinafter referred to as "Halifax Speeches.")
75. Colvin, p. 106.

responsibilities? Heaven knows, I don't want to get back to alliances, but if Germany continues to behave as she has done lately, she may drive us to it. . . . For the moment we must abandon conversations with Germany, we must show our determination not to be bullied by announcing some increase or acceleration in rearmament, and we must quietly and steadily pursue our conversations with Italy. If we can avoid another violent coup in Czechoslovakia, which ought to be feasible, it may be possible for Europe to settle down again, and some day for us to start peace talks again with the Germans.[76]

This statement deserves close scrutiny. Chamberlain readily admits that if Germany continues to behave as she did in Austria, she could be opposed only by alliances outside of the League. Of course, there was no tangible reason to believe that Hitler would change his ways; up to this point he had openly and unilaterally broken numerous treaty provisions. There was every reason to believe that he could not be trusted to keep his word, and even Chamberlain called him "utterly untrustworthy and dishonest." [77] Yet, Chamberlain here claims that he does not want to resort to alliance politics. This statement prompts the inference that he does not want to resort to an alliance with the Soviet Union, the one country whose aid would be essential if "a visible force" were to be mustered to stop Hitler where he was currently expanding, in the east, where Britain and France could show little determination and even less force. Chamberlain's efforts to secure a far-reaching understanding with Germany seem to bely his professed reluctance to engage in alliances. The latter part of the quoted passage reveals how much he still depended on appeasement, to the virtual exclusion of all other alternatives. The key is his wish to avoid a "violent" coup in Czechoslovakia; if the Germans could achieve their ends by any means short of open violence, Chamberlain would approve and could continue talks.

The events of the next week support this analysis. At a

76. Feiling, pp. 341–42.
77. Ibid., p. 354.

Cabinet meeting on March 12 Chamberlain expressed his anger at the German move, but cooled enough to state that "the next question was how we were to prevent an occurrence of similar events in Czechoslovakia." [78] On March 14, Chamberlain condemned Germany's action in a speech before Parliament; however, as Halifax made clear, England would do nothing to oppose the German move,[79] which meant that France could not act and there was no chance for collective security to function. Chamberlain, with the approval of the Cabinet, had decided *not* to show any "determination not to be bullied"; instead of announcing "some increase or acceleration in rearmament," he announced that he would order a "fresh review" of the British defense program.[80] On March 12, still stinging from the impact of Hitler's move, many Cabinet members and British officials became sensitive to Britain's militarily weak position. Even before German troops marched into Austria, Halifax exclaimed to Harvey and Cadogan, "the only thing they understand is force. A warning will be useless unless accompanied by a threat to use force which we cannot do." [81] With Austria out of the way, Cadogan reflected, "we *may* be helpless as regards Czechoslovakia, etc. *That* is what I want to get considered." [82] General Edmund Ironside wrote in his diary on March 13, "The moral for us is that force is the only thing which tells with these two gangsters. If we are not ready to meet this force, then we shall go under. We have had ample warning." [83] One of the primary topics of discussion at the March 12 Cabinet meeting was the "possibility of some expansion and acceleration of our defense forces." The general view was that Air Force and anti-aicraft defenses should receive first priority. However, by the following day the mood of the Cabinet was against any change in armament plans. Simon argued against a change for economic reasons,

78. Colvin, p. 106.
79. Halifax Speeches, p. 127.
80. DBFP, 1: 48; Feiling, p. 342.
81. Harvey, p. 113.
82. Dilks, p. 62.
83. Macloed, p. 49.

and was supported by Thomas Inskip, who asserted that any expansion of the Air Force "would wreck the armaments program recently adopted by the Cabinet." Halifax spoke for prudence in saying that "the events of the last few days had not changed his own opinion as to the German attitude towards Britain. He did not think it could be claimed that a new situation had arisen." Chamberlain simply put off the issue and decided to announce a mere "review of the defense programme." [84] If Chamberlain and Halifax really believed that force was the only thing Hitler understood, they knew that Hitler would not be impressed by the impending "fresh review."

On March 17, Litvinov made a formal statement to the press, describing the new danger faced by the smaller states bordering Germany as well as the larger states. He announced:

> I can therefore state on [behalf of the Soviet Government] that so far as it is concerned it is ready as before to participate in collective actions, which would be decided upon jointly with it and which would aim at checking the further development of aggression and at eliminating the increased danger of a new world war. It is prepared immediately to take up in the League of Nations or outside of it the discussion with other Powers of the practical measures which the circumstances demand. It may be too late tomorrow, but today the time for it is not yet gone if all the States, and the Great Powers in particular, take a firm and unambiguous stand in regard to the problem of the collective salvation of peace.[85]

On the same day, an official version of Litvinov's remarks, identified as representing the views of the Soviet Government, were presented to the British Foreign Office by Soviet Ambassador Maisky.[86]

Adam Ulam's evaluation of this Soviet proposal is worthy of quotation:

84. Colvin, pp. 106–7.
85. Ministry for Foreign Affairs Czechoslovakia and USSR, *New Documents on the History of Munich* (Prague: Orbis, 1958), Doc. No. 4 (Hereinafter referred to as "New Documents.")
86. DBFP, 1, No. 90.

The Soviet move of March 17 is supremely important . . . [in that] it meant exactly what it said. This was no call for a crusade against Hitler, for overthrowing him, or for wresting Austria from his grasp. . . . The note reflected the Soviet belief, which was then shared by many in the West, that a firm enough guarantee of Czechoslovakia by the three Great Powers would make Hitler back down.[87]

I would add one further observation to Ulam's analysis. Doubtlessly, Stalin hoped that a three-power guarantee of Czechoslovakia would deter Hitler; however, he was also anticipating the contingency that Hitler might still risk war over the Sudetens. The critical part of the Litvinov proposal is the declaration of readiness to discuss "practical measures which the circumstances demand." The circumstances had already been described in the proposal: Czechoslovakia was the country now directly threatened. Furthermore, Litvinov claimed to make the proposal, in part, because of his country's responsibilities under treaties with France and Czechoslovakia.[88] Thus, the discussion of "practical measures" for the possible defense of Czechoslovakia could mean only one thing: arranging for the passage of Soviet troops through Eastern Europe. For the countries involved, especially Poland and Rumania, this was seen as a fate worse than Nazi domination. There is no doubt that arms would have to be twisted before the governments of Eastern Europe would consent to allow Soviet troops on their soil; there is also no doubt who would have to do the arm-twisting—Britain and France.

In the next six months, Britain and France would obligingly twist many arms to force a small nation to do something utterly against its will and destructive of its independence. They did it not to secure an alliance with Russia, but rather to satisfy every demand of Hitler.

The Soviet proposal for collective action, with the provision for working outside of the League, was really what Chamberlain, in his March 13 diary entry, admitted was "the only argument

87. Ulam, p. 253.
88. New Documents, No. 4.

Germany understands." Yet, as early as March 14, in his speech before Parliament, Chamberlain revealed his determination not to stand up to Hitler. On March 20, he recorded his despair at the world situation. Of the Russians, whose proposal was then in British hands, he could say nothing more that that they were clandestinely trying to involve England in a war with Germany. He admitted that he had entertained the idea of a "Grand Alliance," but rejected it because it was not practicable. "You have only to look at the map," he wrote, "to see that nothing that France or we could do could possibly save Czechoslovakia, from being overrun by the Germans, if they wanted to do it. . . . Russia is 100 miles away." [89] That England and France could do nothing for Czechoslovakia was obvious; what Chamberlain did not mention with regard to Russia is that she was the only country who could conceivably send troops to Czechoslovakia. The crucial observation was not that Russia was 100 miles away, but that permission would have to be secured before her troops could travel across those 100 miles. Even at that, her air force was stronger than Germany's and Chamberlain himself had been a strong advocate of the decisive influence of air power in the "next war." Yet there is no indication that Chamberlain evaluated any of these military considerations.[90] He concluded his self-serving analysis of March 20 with these lines: "I have therefore abandoned any idea of giving guarantees to Czechoslovakia, or the French in connection with her obligations to that country." [91]

The formal British reply to the Soviet proposal was nothing better than an indelicate snub. Dated March 24, it rejected Litvinov's˙ suggestions for determining "the practical measures required to check the further development of aggression, and to counteract so far as possible the increasing danger of war." The reply expressed Britain's "warm" wish for an international conference at which "all European states would consent to be

89. Feiling, pp. 347–48.
90. Churchill, pp. 274–75.
91. Feiling, p. 348.

represented." This, of course, was an impossibility with Hitler and Mussolini in power. The following lines were a clear insult to the Soviets:

> In the present circumstances, however, it would not appear that such a meeting could be arranged. A conference only attended by some of the European Powers, and designed less to secure the settlement of outstanding problems than to organize concerted action against aggression, would not necessarily, in the view of His Majesty's Government, have such a favorable effect upon the prospects of European peace.[92]

Furthermore, that same day, in explaining the British reply in the House of Commons, Chamberlain asserted that the Soviet plan would "aggravate the tendency towards the establishment of exclusive groups of nations which must . . . be inimical to the prospects of European peace." [93] The thrust of the British position is quite apparent: the Soviet Union is not a European power and must not be permitted to become one. There is simply no other way to reconcile the contradiction inherent in the British position: on the one hand striving for a four-power understanding between Britain, Germany, France, and Italy, *excluding Russia,* and on the other, rejecting the Russian proposal on the basis that it would tend to create "exclusive groups of nations."

British policy after the Anschluss followed two lines. The first was to more seriously pursue negotiations with Italy for the purpose of driving Mussolini away from Hitler and weakening the Axis. The negotiations, which had begun in earnest in February 1938 after Eden's resignation, were concluded on April 16 with an agreement to settle all matters dividing England and Italy, dependent on Italy's withdrawal from Spain. Chamberlain rejoiced that "the Anschluss and the Anglo-Italian agreement together have given the Rome-Berlin axis a nasty jar." [94] The

92. Documents and Materials, No. 7.
93. Churchill, p. 275; Halifax Speeches, pp. 134–35.
94. Feiling, p. 354.

second line of policy was to assure the peaceful settlement of Hitler's claims against Czechoslovakia and the Sudeten Germans, given Chamberlain's determination not to go to war over the Czechs. In the immediate aftermath of the Austrian invasion, the Cabinet looked toward the future and discerned two basic policy alternatives: Britain could assume new responsibilities toward Czechoslovakia, which would entail accelerated rearmament and new defensive alliances, or she could work to help Germany achieve her aims in Central Europe without war. At a meeting of the sub-Cabinet Foreign Affairs Committee Halifax presented the choice as one between full mobilization on the one hand and taking a firm attitude with France that "she would be well advised to exert her influence in Prague in favour of an accommodation" on the other. Chamberlain spoke strongly in favor of the latter alternative, stressing the difficulty of aiding Czechoslovakia in the event of war and arguing that "if Germany could obtain her desiderata by peaceful methods, there is no reason to suppose that she would reject such a procedure in favour of violence." [95] Halifax also favored pressuring Prague, and in a position paper dated March 18 he argued against new commitments to Czechoslovakia directly or through a treaty network with France or Russia, for such a course would involve an acceleration of rearmament and perhaps turn the economy over to a war basis.[96] By April 1, Halifax was holding conversations with his assistants as to "what concessions we might urge on Czech Government to make to Sudeten." [97] "It was thus a foregone conclusion," writes one historian, "when Anglo-French talks in London on 28–29 April produced a decision to put pressure on [Czech President] Benes to settle the Sudeten question." [98] On May 4, Halifax instructed Henderson to inquire, for British consideration, about "the lines of a settlement which in [the German] view would be satisfac-

95. Colvin, pp. 109–10.
96. Keith Middlemas, *Diplomacy of Illusion* (London: Weidenfeld and Nicolson, 1972), pp. 184–87; Harvey, p. 121.
97. Harvey, p. 125.
98. Thorne, p. 61; Churchill, p. 285.

tory to the Sudeten Deutsch." [99] Privately, the British let the Germans know that they would allow the cession of the Sudetenland to Germany provided it was accomplished without violence. "As in the case of Austria, therefore," the above-quoted historian writes, "Hitler was encouraged by Britain to satisfy the growing clamour of Nazis outside the Reich." [100] By the end of April, the British and French Governments became principals in the Czech question, and their object, writes A. J. P. Taylor, "however disguised, was to exact concessions from the Czechs, not to restrain Germany." [101]

On April 23, while the French and British pondered how to persuade Benes to accede to German demands, Stalin informed the Czechs: "If requested, the U.S.S.R. is prepared—in agreement with France and Czechoslovakia—to take all necessary measures relating to the security of Czechoslovakia. She disposes of all necessary means for doing so." [102] On May 12, Litviniv discussed the Czech question with Bonnet in a meeting at Geneva. In response to a question from Bonnet as to how Russia could aid Czechoslovakia in view of the Polish and Rumanian refusal to allow the passage of Soviet troops, Litvinov asserted that, in view of the lack of Soviet influence in these countries, it was necessary that France obtain permission for this. Litvinov also suggested just military talks between Soviet, French, and Czech general staffs. Bonnet indicated that he accepted the current negative position of Poland and Rumania, and the talk terminated.[103] There can be no doubt about the vehemence of the Polish and Rumanian refusal to permit the passage of Soviet troops; both countries informed Bonnet at Geneva in May that such an attempt would provoke an immediate declaration of war against the Soviet Union. The Polish Ambassador to France told William Bullitt that if Soviet planes flew over Poland en route to Czechoslovakia they would be

99. DBFP, 1, No. 172.
100. Thorne, p. 62.
101. Taylor, p. 161.
102. New Documents, No. 7.
103. Ibid., No. 14.

attacked by the Polish air force.[104] Regardless of this opposition, as Tayor correctly notes, "it was indeed no part of Bonnet's policy to make Soviet intervention possible." [105] Quite the contrary, Bonnet wished to *prevent* Soviet intervention. On July 26, 1938, he told William Bullitt and Henry Morganthau that he was

> attempting to obtain assurance from the Soviet Government that if war should come in Central Europe the Soviet Union would positively not attempt to march armies across the territories of Poland and Rumania and would not send airplanes across those territories but would confine its assistance to the furnishing of munitions and implements of war to the Polish and Rumanian Governments.[106]

France, following Britain's lead, was determined to avoid war at all costs. The history of the events culminating in the Munich agreement is vitally important in understanding the Cold War.

The Czech crisis seemed to come to a head on May 20 when widespread rumors of German troop movements at the Czech border were met by partial Czech mobilization. Immediately Britain and France announced their intention to stand by Czechoslovakia. Bonnet declared that France would "provide the utmost help" if Czechoslovakia were attacked, and Halifax warned Ribbentrop that "if from any precipitate action" a general conflict were to ensue, Britain should not be counted on to stand aside.[107] These were empty promises, as both governments realized. During the weekend crisis following May 20, Bonnet urged the Czechs to halt their mobilization and assured the British Ambassador, Phipps, that "if Czechoslovakia were really unreasonable the French Government might well declare that France considered herself released from her bond. Furthermore, Bonnet stated "that he would readily put any pressure on

104. McSherry, pp. 75–76.
105. Taylor, p. 164.
106. FRUS, 1938, I, p. 58.
107. Thorne, p. 63.

Czech Government that you [Halifax] might think at any moment desirable in order to ensure a peaceful settlement of the Sudeten question." [108] This French position was in response to the warning from Halifax, dated May 22, that, "If . . . the French Government were to assume that His Majesty's Government would at once take joint military action with them to preserve Czechoslovakia against German aggression, it is only fair to warn them that our statements do not warrant any such assumption." [109] Also, as one historian notes, "it is difficult . . . to avoid the word servility when describing British dealings with Berlin in this period." [110] On June 1 Henderson told German State Secretary Weizacker that Britain and France had warned Prague that they would abandon her if she would not listen to reason.[111]

The British were now feeling the heat. They expected Hitler to act, but were not sure when. They deduced that September 12 would be the earliest date, and the object of their policy was to force Benes, before September 12, to make the decisive concessions which they felt alone could deter war.[112] Chamberlain groped for a solution, wishing to avoid for the British the task of coercing Benes. Ultimately, he had to force a British "mediator" on Prague. On July 26, he sent Lord Runciman to Czechoslovakia to work out the German-Czech problem. In announcing the mission in the House of Commons on that date, Chamberlain, in the words of one historian, "lied brazenly and deliberately" by declaring that Prague had requested a mediator and denying that Britain had interfered in the internal affairs of Czechoslovakia.[113] Another prominent historian of the Munich period has called Chamberlain's speech "as remarkable an example of prevarication as that Chamber can ever have heard." [114]

108. DBFP, 1: 357.
109. Ibid., p. 347.
110. Thorne, p. 64.
111. DGFP, 2, No. 233.
112. Taylor, p. 167.
113. Fleming, p. 72.
114. John W. Wheeler-Bennett, *Munich: Proloogue to Tragedy* (New York: Duell, Sloan and Pearce, 1963), pp. 74–76.

Benes, however, outmaneuvered Runciman by calling in the Sudeten leaders on September 4 and promising to give in to their every demand. This concession by Benes undermined the very pretext by which Hitler planned to make war on Czechoslovakia. As Taylor writes, "The Sudeten Germans had a good case: they did not possess national equality. . . . By September, thanks to Benes, the bottom had been knocked out of this case." [115] September 12 did not bring the German aggression anticipated by Britain, but on that date Hitler did make a speech demanding the remedy of all Sudeten grievances, and the next day, the Sudeten leaders broke off their negotiations with Benes and gave the signal for a revolt, which might have been used by Hitler as a pretext for intervention. Again, Benes succeeded. Within 24 hours, he restored order and demonstrated his authority over his entire country.

While Runciman was pressuring Benes, the Soviets affirmed their treaty obligations to Czechoslovakia. On September 2, in response to a query by the French, Litvinov pledged that the Soviets would fulfill their treaty commitments, which obliged them to act in the event that France acted first. As to how the Soviets intended to fulfill their commitments should the situation arise, Litvinov proposed immediate talks between France, Czechoslovakia, and Russia, and suggested that "in view of the negative attitude adopted by Warsaw and Bucharest he could see only one practical step," an appeal to the League of Nations under Article XI to secure the right of passage for Soviet troops through Poland and Rumania. [116] The very idea that Czechoslovakia's plight be brought before the League struck fear in the hearts of the British and French, for such a move would have undercut any efforts at accommodating Hitler. Thus, Bonnet suppressed this element of the Soviet reply. [117] On September 11, Bonnet saw Litvinov personally at Geneva, where the latter

115. Taylor, p. 170; Churchill, p. 299.
116. New Documents, Nos. 26, 27, 30; Taylor, p. 172; Max Beloff, *The Foreign Policy of Soviet Russia, 1929–1941*, vol. 2 (London: Oxford University Press, 1949): 143.
117. Thorne, p. 70.

again raised the issue and said "that he would like to get the Czech question discussed by an ad hoc committee." Bonnet and R. A. Butler, from the British Foreign Office, discouraged the idea; "Let us hope no more will come of this idea," Butler wired home.[118] Officially, the British ignored the Soviet proposal.[119]

Whether the Soviets were sincere in pledging to fulfill their treaty commitments is academic. An early historian of Soviet foreign policy, Max Beloff, has asserted that there is "very little evidence" that the Soviet Government "was preparing its own people for the possibility that it would itself be involved in war" over Czechoslovakia. Beloff suggests that "the Soviet Union was certain from very early on that France and Great Britain would not fight for Czechoslovakia and that Czechoslovakia would not resist without their support." [120] Fontaine takes a similar position; in reference to the Soviet pledges of September 1938 he asks "what good were these words if the man who spoke them was convinced that France would not make a move?" [121] There is some substance in the skeptical view that the only reason the Soviets pledged to fulfill their commitments to Czechoslovakia is that they firmly believed they would never have the opportunity to do so. Still, one can not overlook certain considerations: 1) the Soviets made proposals for measures that were clearly not required of them under the terms of their treaties with France and Czechoslovakia, such as concerted action including Britain; 2) in view of the Soviet attitude toward the League, it would seem that Litvinov's proposal to bring the Czech problem to the attention of the League was calculated to put pressure on the British and French to reach some understanding with Russia, and 3) the Soviets really had nothing to gain by making the proposals they did, and, in fact, stood to lose if they were insincere and Britain and France decided to "call their bluff." The Soviet position and conduct, whatever

118. DBFP, 3, No. 835.
119. Churchill, pp. 304–5.
120. Beloff, p. 166.
121. Fontaine, p. 93.

its sincerity, is irreproachable. They repeatedly opted for a joint conference between Britain, France, and the U.S.S.R. "with a view to publishing a declaration which may serve to prevent an attack by Germany on Czechoslovakia." [122] In the event this failed, they stated their willingness to enter into military staff discussions, which were a necessary first step to fulfilling the Franco-Soviet and Czech-Soviet treaties. In short, the Russians did all they could; it was up to France to agree to the military talks suggested by Moscow, and it was inconceivable that any governments except those of France or Britain could apply the diplomatic pressure necessary to secure the right of passage for Soviet troops through Poland and Rumania.

Yet, while France publicly clung to her treaties with Moscow and Prague as vital elements in her foreign policy, privately she "was desperately anxious for a possible way out of this 'impasse' without being *obliged* to fight."[123] By September 13, with the Sudetens in revolt, Bonnet told the British Ambassador Phipps that "peace must be preserved at any price." [124]

On September 11, Chamberlain wrote of his opposition to the theory that German aggression could be stopped by the threat of force, based on his unwillingness to go to war over a country in which Britain was not vitally interested. He added that "another consideration" in his decision not to risk war with Hitler involved a "plan" he had:

> The time for this has not yet arrived, and it is always possible that Hitler might act so unexpectedly as to forestall it. That is a risk which we have to take, but in the meantime I do not want to do anything which would destroy its chance of success because, if it came off, it would go far beyond the present crisis, and might prove the opportunity for bringing about a complete change in the international situation.[125]

What Chamberlain had in mind was to grant all of Hitler's

122. New Documents, No. 30.
123. DBFP, 2, No. 834.
124. Ibid., No. 855.
125. Feiling, p. 361.

demands toward Czechoslovakia, including separation of the Sudetenland without a plebiscite, with a view toward resuming efforts for an Anglo-German understanding. On September 13 the French Cabinet voted against war, and Bonnet confessed his desperation for anything that would preserve peace. This gave Chamberlain the opportunity to act. The same day he wrote to Hitler, offering to fly to Germany overnight for personal negotiations.[126] Hitler accepted, and on September 15 the two leaders were conferring at Berchtesgaden.

It was at this meeting that Chamberlain sealed Czechoslovakia's fate. He conceded the principal of detachment of the Sudetenland and made it his mandate to secure the approval of his colleagues and the French. As Taylor points out, "he did not enquire whether a truncated Czechoslovakia could remain independent or what the strategic consequences would be for the Western powers; he did not consider how the national composition of Czechoslovakia could be ascertained." [127] In effect, the Czechs were expected not only "to surrender territory which they firmly held so that France could escape war," [128] but also "to abolish political liberties, suppress free speech . . . relinquish her tie with France and Soviet Russia, give up her responsibilities as a 'grown up' member of the League . . . accept a guarantee by the 'principal powers,' and enter the German economic system." [129]

After securing agreement among his colleagues and the French Government, Chamberlain presented his terms to Prague on September 19: The Czechs would automatically cede all areas with over 50 percent German population to the Reich, with boundaries in question to be settled at a later date and possibly guaranteed by all bordering countries and Britain and France.[130] At the same time, the British tried to prevent the Czechs from mobilizing.[131] Cadogan thought these terms "pretty

126. Ibid., p. 363.
127. Taylor, p. 174.
128. Ibid., p. 175.
129. Thorne, p. 73.
130. Wheeler-Bennett, Appendix I; New Documents, No. 35.
131. DBFP, 2, No. 927.

stiff—telling him to surrender!"[132] The Benes Government was in an untenable position, having to choose between the dismemberment of its country or an invasion that it could not withstand alone. After receiving the Anglo-French proposals, Benes urgently inquired of the French and Soviet Governments whether they would fulfill their treaty commitments to Czechoslovakia in the event of war; he also asked the Soviets if they would come to the aid of his country under Articles 16 and 17 of the League covenant.[133] The next day, the Soviet Government conveyed the following message to Prague:

> With France remaining loyal to the pact, is the U.S.S.R. resolved to help instantly and effectively? The Government replies Yes, instantly and effectively, To the second question, whether in the event of an appeal being made to the League of Nations, the U.S.S.R. is willing to fulfill its duties according to Articles 16 and 17, the Government replied Yes, in every respect.[134]

The same day, September 20, Benes rejected the Anglo-French proposals. It is doubtful that he did so because he accepted the Soviet assurance, but rather because he was counting on France's aid at the last minute.[135]

Faced with Benes's intransigence, the British and the French quickly delivered an ultimatum to the Czech Government. The Czechs were curtly informed that England would not go to war and, if war should break out, France "will not fulfill her treaty obligations"; if the Government persisted in its refusal to accept the terms offered, "she would bear the responsibility for the war."[136] Prague accepted, and the government of Premier Hozda resigned in shame.[137]

When Chamberlain met again with Hitler at Godesberg, Hitler declared that the previous proposals were no longer

132. Dilks, p. 100.
133. New Documents, No. 36.
134. Ibid., No. 39.
135. Taylor, p. 178.
136. New Documents, No. 42.
137. Thorne, pp. 75–76.

sufficient, and that German troops must occupy Czech territory by October 1. Why Hitler made this new demand is not relevant to this study, and is open to question. He may have wanted to provoke war. Taylor has suggested that Hitler's position was altered by the demands of Poland and Hungary for similar concessions for their minorities in the Tesin and Slovakia regions of Czechoslovakia.[138] It is true that Poland and Hungary were hovering overhead like vultures, as Churchill described them, anxious to pick at the carcass of what was once Czechoslovakia.[139] Nevertheless, Chamberlain rejected Hitler's ultimatum on September 23; he could not agree to an outright invasion of Czechoslovakia. The British and the French, still determined to avoid war, had to come up with some compromise acceptable to Hitler. In the first few days following the 23rd this seemed impossible, and war seemed imminent. Halifax, against Chamberlain's wish, told the Czechs that there could no longer be any objection to their mobilizing.[140] Britain mobilized her fleet, and France called up two categories of her reserves, only about half a million men.[141] The Russians informed the French and the Czechs that thirty infantry divisions, reinforced with reservists, had been drawn up at her Western frontiers, and that aviation and tank units "are in full readiness." [142]

The British at first went overboard in their declarations to stand by Czechoslovakia. At Churchill's urging, on September 26, the Foreign Office issued a communiqué stating that if Germany attacked Czechoslovakia, "France will be bound to come to her assistance, and Great Britain and Russia will certainly stand by France." [143] Yet, neither France nor Russia had been consulted in advance, and Bonnet denounced the communiqué as a forgery.[144] The same day, Horace Wilson delivered a

138. Taylor, pp. 179–80.
139. Churchill, p. 322.
140. Taylor, p. 180.
141. Feiling, p. 371.
142. New Documents, No. 53.
143. Churchill, p. 309.
144. Feiling, p. 371; Taylor, p. 182.

special message from Chamberlain to Hitler, in which the British repeated France's intention to fight for Czechoslovakia and Britain's obligation to support the French.[145]

There are several indications that the Soviets expected a change in Anglo-French policy in the days following September 22. In a letter of September 23, a British representative at Geneva, Robert Boothby, summarized a conversation with Litvinov. The Soviet Foreign Minister told Boothby that he had been in touch with the Czechs during the previous week and had assured them that in the event of an attack by Germany, Russia "would give them effective aid. Help in the air would certainly be given, but it was more doubtful whether it could be given on land." [146] There is evidence that the Russians sent hundreds of planes to Czechoslovakia during September.[147] On the 23rd, Halifax wired Butler at Geneva with instructions to contact Litvinov and inquire about the intentions of the Soviet Government. Litvinov repeated the pledge that Russia would come to the aid of Czechoslovakia if France did; however, he seemed to attach a new significance to this British overture:

> He said he welcomed the fact we had asked him to talk to us. He had for long been hoping for conversations between Great Britain, France and Russia, and he would like to suggest to us in this informal conversation that a meeting of the three Powers mentioned, together with Rumania and any other small Power who could be regarded as reliable, should take place away from the atmosphere of Geneva . . . and so show the Germans that we mean business. . . . He would be ready then to discuss military and air questions.[148]

Furthermore, Litvinov told his British associates, in confidence, that the Soviet Government had informed Poland that if the latter attacked Czechoslovakia, the "pact of non-aggression existing between Poland and Russia would automatically lapse and

145. DBFP, 2, No. 1129.
146. Middlemas, p. 381.
147. Beloff, p. 160.
148. DBFP, 2: 498.

Russia would take actions." [149] Max Beloff writes that "foreign observers in Moscow began to see signs of definite intentions to act on the part of the Soviet Government." On September 26, the same day that the British Foreign Office issued a warning to Germany that mentioned Russia, the Soviets announced for the first time in public that Poland had been warned not to attack Czechoslovakia; also published was the text of the Czech-Soviet treaty, emphasizing Russia's obligation to aid Czechoslovakia.[150]

As in May, the British were insincere in their pledges. Chamberlain and Wilson were willing to accept the Godesberg terms [151] and Chamberlain's central problem was to arrange his acceptance in such a way as to keep Hitler from making war while not losing the popular support of the British people. In this context, all the components of the war scare following September 22 actually helped Chamberlain gain acceptance for Hitler's harsher demands because the British people now came to feel the flames of war grow so hot that they would accept almost anything to extinguish them. The British had no confidence in France's ability to wage war against Germany, and on September 27 Halifax urged the French not to move if Czechoslovakia were invaded.[152] Bonnet could not have agreed more: "France will not fight with any heart in a hopeless offensive war against Germany, for which she is not prepared." [153] That evening, Chamberlain addressed the British people and spoke in general terms of avoiding war. After his talk, he received a message from Hitler which seemed to offer the possibility of a peaceful settlement. In his response, Chamberlain offered to come to Berlin to settle the issue with French and Italian representatives, assuring Hitler that "you can get all the essentials without war, and without delay." [154] Simultaneously he sent a personal appeal to Mussolini. The following day he was

149. Ibid.
150. Beloff, pp. 159–60.
151. Thorne, pp. 77–78; Dilks, p. 103; Birkenhead, pp. 399–401.
152. DBFP, 2, No. 1143.
153. Ibid., No. 1160.
154. Feiling, p. 372.

able to announce in the Commons that the four powers, Britain, France, Germany, and Italy were to meet at Munich.

Russia, which had an unmistakable interest in the settlement of the Czech question, was not invited to the Munich meeting. One could devote pages to this apparent diplomatic outrage. Yet, the essential observation is that Chamberlain could never have arranged the meeting had there been the slightest chance that Russia would be invited.[155] Chamberlain wanted to accommodate Hitler, which meant excluding Russia from European affairs. As Deutscher has explained, "the unwritten maxim of Munich was to keep Russia out of Europe." [156] At the Nuremberg trials, Marshal Keitel testified that Germany would not have attacked Czechoslovakia in 1938 had the Western Powers backed Prague. "The object of Munich," he said, "was to get Russia out of Europe, to gain time, and to complete the German armaments." [157] As for Chamberlain's and Halifax's motivation, I note the provocative statement by André Fontaine: "It was their anti-Soviet prejudices much more than fear of war that explains the whole policy that led to Munich." [158] I believe that this interpretation makes a vital distinction that helps clarify the rather tenuous assessment of the meaning of Russia's exclusion at Munich that some historians have advanced. There can be little doubt that the British policy that *led* to Munich was based, in part, on anti-Bolshevism and fear of the Soviet Union; it was also based on a fear of war, an unwillingness to undertake the preparations for war, and a desire to restructure Europe. This was a policy evolved over a period of years, usually not in the midst of crises, and never at a stage where war appeared imminent in a matter of days. By the time of the Godesberg ultimatum of September 22, 1938, the exclusion of Russia from Europe was merely an assumed aspect of the general policy that Chamberlain sought

155. This was Halifax's argument to the House of Lords on September 29, 1938. (Birkenhead, p. 408.)
156. Deutscher, p. 427.
157. Churchill, p. 319.
158. Fontaine, p. 63.

to pursue. The week following September 22 was a period of great crisis, and the immediate need of the British, as formulated by Chamberlain and Halifax, was to avoid war. Munich was a last-ditch effort to prevent war and, at the same time, to salvage the whole policy of appeasement. The British did not exclude the Soviet Union from Europe *at the time of Munich;* they did this long before the Czech crisis, and at Munich they merely reaffirmed their determination to keep Soviet Russia detached from European affairs by actively pursuing a new European order dictated by Hitler.

The Czechs fared little better than the Soviets; their representatives were present at Munich, but excluded from the four-power talks. The negotiations were relatively brief, and at 2 A.M. on September 30, a memorandum was drawn up and signed that reflected "in essentials the acceptance of the Godesberg ultimatum." [159] Stripped of some of the more brutal aspects of Hitler's stiff terms, it still provided for military occupation in five stages, beginning October 1 and to be completed in 10 days. [160] The Czech representatives were shown the agreement after it had been signed, and were given until 5 P.M. that day to accept or take the consequences of rejection. Of course, there was no choice. The Czechs accepted and Benes resigned.

Chamberlain, at his initiative, met alone with Hitler on September 30. The two leaders discussed some outstanding issues between their countries, such as disarmament and economic relations with Southeast Europe. At the end of the meeting, Chamberlain produced a declaration that he had prepared earlier and asked Hitler to sign it, which the latter did eagerly. [161] The Declaration read as follows:

> We, the German Führer and Chancellor, and the British Prime Minister . . . are agreed in recognizing that the question of Anglo-German relations is of the first importance for the two countries and for Europe.

159. Churchill, p. 317.
160. Feiling, p. 378.
161. Ibid., pp. 376–77.

We regard the agreement signed last night, and the Anglo-German Naval agreement, as symbolic of the desire of our two peoples never to go to war with one another again.

We are resolved that the method of consultation shall be the method adopted to deal with any other questions that may concern our two countries, and we are determined to continue our efforts to remove possible sources of differences, and thus to contribute to assure the peace of Europe.[162]

In short, the declaration affirmed that Britain's policy would remain the same with respect to seeking an understanding with Germany, and added Hitler's approval of and apparent cooperation with the policy.

Halifax outlined the philosophy behind Britain's post-Munich foreign policy in answer to a request from Ambassador Phipps for the British Government's attitude toward France's efforts to improve her relationship with Germany. Halifax's discussion is illuminating and deserves lengthy quotation:

> Hence forward we must count with German predominance in Central Europe. . . .
> In these conditions it seems to me that Great Britain and France have to uphold *their* predominant position in Western Europe by the maintenance of such armed strength as would render any attack upon them hazardous. They should also firmly maintain their hold on the Mediterranean and the Near East. . . .
> The greatest lesson of the crisis has been the unwisdom of basing a foreign policy on insufficient armed strength. . . .
> It is one thing to allow German expansion in Central Europe, which to my mind is a normal and natural thing, but we must be able to resist German expansion in Western Europe or else our whole position is undermined. . . .
> The immediate future must necessarily be a time of more of the painful readjustments to the new realities in Europe. While my broad conclusion is that we shall see Germany consolidate herself in Central Europe, with Great Britain and France doing the same in Western Europe, the Mediterranean and overseas, certain factors remain obscure. What is to be the role of Poland and of Soviet Russia? If the Poland of

162. Ibid., p. 381.

Beck . . . can never ally herself with Soviet Russia, and if France . . . relaxes her alliance with Poland the latter can presumably only fall more and more into the German orbit. Soviet Russia, on the other hand, can scarcely become the ally of Germany so long as Hitler lives, although there are obvious economic reasons for bringing them together; she may choose to go into isolation or else she may prefer to maintain contact with the Western Powers through the French alliance.

There is also the problem raised by possible German expansion into the Ukraine. Subject only to the consideration that I should hope France would protect herself—and us—from being entangled by Russia in war with Germany, I should hesitate to advise the French Government to denounce the Franco-Soviet pact as the future is still far too uncertain! Russia, for good or for evil, is part of Europe and we cannot ignore her existence.

Finally . . . although we do not expect to detach Italy from the Axis, we believe the [Anglo-Italian] Agreement will increase Mussolini's power of maneuver and so make him less dependent on Hitler, and therefore freer to resume the classic Italian role of balancing between Germany and the Western Powers.[163]

This document is startling in its frank but hopelessly self-serving analysis. Acceptance of German predominance in Central Europe had been and would have to be the sine qua non of a policy of cooperation with Hitler. Churchill wrote of Chamberlain on November 17, "he believes that he can make a good settlement for Europe and for the British Empire by coming to terms with Herr Hitler and Signor Mussolini."[164] Halifax clearly defined the areas of interest to Britain: Western Europe, the Mediterranean, and her colonies. France was the key to Britain's position in Western Europe, because she would inevitably bear the heaviest burden if Hitler ever struck in the West. A rearmed and independent France was vital to Britain, Halifax wrote, because without French resistance, "we might have to face alone the full weight of German military power in the West."[165]

163. Halifax to Phipps, November 1, 1938, DBFP, 3: 252–53.
164. Churchill, p. 333.
165. DBFP, 3: 252–53.

British policy was thus based on three interrelated assumptions: (1) sufficient military power to *deter* an attack on any area of British interest, (2) fulfilling, to the degree possible, Hitler's terms, and (3) maintaining friendly relations with Mussolini to have some means of restraining Hitler; these three factors would preserve peace and insure the development of a new status quo in which British interests, largely commercial and economic, could thrive.

Halifax had stressed the first two of these assumptions with brutal frankness in a discussion with American Ambassador Kennedy on October 12. He stated that there was no point in fighting Germany unless Hitler directly interfered with Britain or her colonies. To deter the risk of war against her vital interests, Britain should build up her air strength. Kennedy's report continues:

> After that . . . let Hitler go ahead and do what he likes in Central Europe. In other words, there is no question in Halifax's mind that reasonably soon Hitler will make a start for Danzig, with Polish concurrence, and then for Memel, with Lithuanian acquiescence, and even if he decides to go into Rumania it is Halifax's idea that England would never have got into the Czechoslovak situation if it had not been for France.[166]

Eastern Europe and Russia were the snags in the British plan. Halifax's suspicion that Poland would fall more into the German orbit was justified at the time, and he was absolutely correct in presuming that Hitler would soon "make a start for Danzig"; Ribbentrop began pressing German claims to Danzig in discussions with the Polish Ambassador on October 24.[167] However, his analysis of Russia's position is naive and self-serving. Halifax knew that Russia was "part of Europe," but he was apparently unwilling to admit that she had any national interests to protect; to him, Russia existed only insofar as she

166. FRUS (1938), 1: 85–86.
167. McSherry, pp. 113–14.

could be of service to Britain or France. When Halifax wrote of the impossibility of a Nazi-Soviet alliance, he did not have in mind an alliance *against* Britain and France, but rather one that would *benefit* the two Western nations, as he made obvious in his follow-up statement that "there are obvious economic reasons for bringing them together." Although the British were against political cooperation with Soviet Russia, they freely acknowledged the value of commercial cooperation; Russia was a huge market. If she could somehow be integrated into the European economic community through an understanding with a powerful and predominant Nazi Germany, the economic benefits could be great. Of course, Halifax realized that this was not a possibility. What, then, was Soviet Russia to do, faced with a hostile and expansionist Germany whose predominance in Central Europe was openly encouraged and facilitated by Britain and France and whose domination of Eastern Europe seemed inevitable either through military action, internal subversion of Nazi fifth columns, or economic assimilation, none of which the West and the East European governments could be depended upon to resist? What was Russia to do when she shared a border with the maniacal German leader who had justified so much of his foreign policy on the basis of the "Soviet threat" and his violent anti-Bolshevism? Indeed, could Russia tolerate having any of her bordering states, particularly Poland, allied with or subservient to Germany? Obviously, Russia had to protect herself; it would not have taken any elaborate intelligence operation to discern that after Munich, one of the vital objectives of Soviet diplomacy would be to seek such protection, which meant, in any case, active Soviet opposition to the European order Britain was trying to create. Indeed, on November 26, 1938, Russia signed an agreement with Poland reaffirming the 1932 Polish-Soviet Nonaggression Pact. As Ulam has written, "the prospect of Poland becoming a German Satellite or being conquered by Germany had to be viewed as a mortal danger to the Soviet Union." [168]

168. Ulam, pp. 260–61.

In this context, Halifax's conjecture about the future courses of Soviet policy is a striking example of blindness caused by wishful thinking. Russia could either isolate herself or keep in touch with the West "through the French alliance," he deduced. One wonders if, when Halifax wrote that Russia could "choose to go into isolation," he anticipated that the Soviet leaders might physically move their country to a new location, for otherwise there was no way that Moscow could "isolate" Russia from Europe. It is particularly revealing that Halifax, who had encouraged France to break her treaty with Moscow and Prague and who had thus completely undermined the tenuous system of alliances that Russia had built in her defense, could really believe that Russia would still depend on her alliance with France. The British attitude is further revealed by Halifax's advice that France not denounce her alliance with Russia because of possible unforeseen future contingencies, provided that France not allow Russia to use the alliance to draw the West into a war with Germany. Taylor has concisely translated this passage of Halifax's letter: "In plain English: Russia should fight for British interests, but Great Britain and France should not fight for hers." [169] It should be noted that Halifax invoked the Franco-Soviet alliance in reference to German expansion into the Ukraine. The clear implication of his letter to Phipps, stated more openly in conversation with Joseph Kennedy, is that Britain and France should not fight for the Ukraine unless Hitler made it untenable for them to stand aside, that is, if he engaged in "unprovoked aggression" against that region.

The British were anxious to let the Germans know that they still sought a comprehensive agreement, and suggestions of this nature were made even during the sensitive maneuverings at the height of the Munich crisis. Sir Horace Wilson met with Hitler, Ribbentrop, and Henderson in Berlin on September 27, 1938, the day before the four powers agreed to meet at Munich. Wilson spoke openly with Hitler:

169. Taylor, p. 197.

Many Englishmen, and he was one of them, wished heartily to enter into a discussion with Germany on all questions outstanding between the two countries. . . . In the opinion of the British, a period of great economic prosperity throughout the world must result from the settlement of all these questions. On the British side there was also the earnest desire for a discussion and an agreement with Germany. He, Sir Horace, remembered that the Führer had once described Britain and Germany as bulwarks against the forces of destruction, particularly from the East. He himself and many other Englishmen had not forgotten these words.[170]

On October 7, Halifax met with the German Ambassador in London, Herbert von Dirksen, and expressed his hope that "a further extension of the basis for Anglo-German relations found in the Munich conference between the Führer and Chamberlain would shortly be made possible." Halifax, however, was quite sensitive to the importance of public opinion in enabling the British Government to carry out the policy it desired; thus he was disturbed at reports in the British press about the ill-treatment of Sudetens by the Germans. At this meeting he told Dirksen "he would be grateful if by means of relevant German reports he might be enabled to combat such assertions, the spreading of which might in fact hamper the advocates of friendly Anglo-German relations in the realization of their aspirations." [171]

On October 18, British Home Secretary Sir Samuel Hoare had a meeting with Dirksen. Hoare spoke of a four-power agreement on a wide range of issues, and then "let slip the observation that, after a further rapprochement between the four European Great Powers, the acceptance of certain defense obligations, or even a guarantee by them against Soviet Russia, was conceivable in the event of an attack by Soviet Russia." [172]

Although the experience of Munich gave many members of the Cabinet, including Halifax, serious second thoughts about the

170. DGFP, 1: 963–65.
171. Ibid., 4, No. 249.
172. Ibid., p. 321.

wisdom of Britain's policy toward Germany and rearmament, Chamberlain seems to have been strengthened in his determination to continue along the same lines. At a Cabinet meeting of October 3, "one view . . . strongly held . . . was that we must never again allow ourselves to be got into the position in which we had been for the last few weeks, and that every effort should be made to intensify our rearmament programme." Halifax expressed his strong support for this view. Chamberlain spoke cautiously, as if to soften his dissent from the general view:

> Ever since he had been Chancellor of the Exchequer he had been oppressed with the sense that the burden of armaments might break our backs. This had led him to try to resolve the causes responsible for the armaments race. We were now in a more hopeful position, he thought. The contacts established with the Dictator Powers opened up the possibility that we might be able to reach some agreement with them that would stop the armaments race. It was clear, however, that it would be madness for the country to stop rearming until we were convinced that other countries would act in the same way. For the time being, therefore, we should relax no particle of effort until our deficiencies had been made good. That, however, was not the same as saying that we would embark on a great increase in our armaments programme.[173]

On October 31, Chamberlain was even more emphatic with the Cabinet:

> Our policy is one of appeasement [he said]. We must aim at establishing relations with the Dictator Powers which will lead to a settlement in Europe and a sense of stability. A good deal of false emphasis has been placed . . . in the country and in the Press . . . on rearmament, as though one result of the Munich Agreement has been that it will be necessary to add to our rearmament programme.[174]

173. Colvin, pp. 170–71.
174. Ibid., p. 173. See also Eden, *The Reckoning* (Boston: Houghton Mifflin Co., 1965), pp. 42–43.

In the early months of 1939, Chamberlain remained content to maintain the same program of rearmament as before Munich; he opposed any effort at expansion or redefinition. At a Cabinet meeting of February 2, 1939, he became disconcerted at a proposal that six army divisions be equipped for a continental role, owing to the unprepared state of the Army for a war on the Continent. Chamberlain argued, "An unanswerable case can be made for increased armaments in every Service, if the financial aspect is ignored, but finance can not be ignored since our financial strength is one of our strongest weapons in any war that is not over in a short time." [175]

Toward the end of November 1938, Oliver Harvey spoke with William Strang about Britain's post-Munich policy, and his diary entry reveals some interesting reflections on Chamberlain's opposition to expanded rearmament. Strang explained Chamberlain's philosophy as

> play for time and avoid fighting at all costs except on a first-class vital British interest. On the other hand, while accepting this reasoning as tenable, W. Strang says the corollary is that we should at the same time re-arm as hard as possible, and that is what the Government and P.M. are not doing. Strang and I agree that the real opposition to re-arming comes from the rich classes in the Party who fear taxation and believe Nazis on the whole are more conservative than Communists and Socialists; any war, whether we win or not, would destroy the rich idle classes and so they are for peace at any price.[176]

Thus, in the winter after Munich, Britain was determined to defend her vital interests, but she had no intention of fighting in Eastern Europe. Accordingly, she almost immediately moved to release herself from the rather ambiguous guarantee of the truncated Czechoslovakia she had made at Munich. In the protocol of the Munich agreement, Britain and France announced that they stood by their original offer for an international guarantee of Czechoslovakia's new borders against unprovoked aggres-

175. Ibid., p. 183.
176. Harvey, p. 222.

sion.[177] Such a guarantee was virtually meaningless, since the penetration of Nazi fifth columns into Czechoslovakia could easily enable Hitler to provoke a situation by which he could "justify" military action. Furthermore, the Anglo-French offer contained as "one of the principle conditions . . . the substitution of a general guarantee . . . in place of existing treaties which involve reciprocal obligations of a military character." [178] In simple terms, the Czechs were asked to renounce their treaties with France and Russia and accept instead a guarantee from Britain, France, Germany, and Italy—with Russia excluded. The chief ambiguity of such a "general guarantee" was whether it was to be invoked collectively or individually. Chamberlain used this loophole to escape from a commitment to Czechoslovakia. In a meeting with the French and British Foreign Ministers in Paris on November 24, Chamberlain interpreted the guarantee as collective only: "He had never conceived of a situation in which Great Britain might have to carry out her obligations alone." [179] Disturbed at Czech nonresponsiveness on the question of the nature of the guarantee, Halifax on December 8 curtly informed the Czechs as follows:

> His Majesty's Government are not prepared to consider a guarantee which might oblige them, alone or with France, to come to the assistance of Czechoslovakia in circumstances in which effective help could not be rendered. This would be the case if either Germany or Italy were the aggressor and the other declined to fulfill the guarantee.[180]

In other words, Germany or Italy held the power to veto any aid in defense of Czechoslovakia; or, to be more concise, in the opinion of the British Government, there was no guarantee.

As Halifax had stated in his letter to Phipps, the British regarded Mussolini's influence as instrumental in controlling Hitler.

177. Wheeler-Bennett, p. 466.
178. Ibid., p. 457.
179. DBFP, 3, No. 325.
180. Ibid., No. 408.

Thus, faced with "the failure of Hitler to make the slightest gesture of friendliness" in the last months of 1938,[181] Britain devoted increasingly more attention to Rome. In October the British pushed for ratification of the Anglo-Italian agreement of April 1938, despite the absence of the required Italian withdrawals from Spain. Ratification was secured, and the agreement signed November 16, but in the process the British Ambassador to Italy, Perth, suffered such abuse that one historian has commented, "Perhaps only Henderson among British diplomats could have rivalled Perth in inviting and accepting such treatment." [182] In early January, Chamberlain flew to Rome for a personal meeting with Mussolini and a chance "to reach the Italian people." The Prime Minister's contemporaneous impression was "that I am satisfied that the journey has definitely strengthened the chances of peace." [183] The Italian Foreign Minister, struck with the weakness evidenced by Chamberlain and Halifax, told Ribbentrop that "the visit was a fiasco," which convinced him of the necessity for a "Triple Alliance" including Japan; with the British engaged in "this somber preoccupation of theirs. . . . we could get whatever we want." [184] In February 1939, Chamberlain recognized General Franco as the legitimate ruler of Spain.[185] No one could dispute the judgment that "the belief that Mussolini could restrain Hitler was misplaced." [186]

Soviet foreign policy during the winter following Munich reflected a careful search for security on Russia's Western frontier. Munich had undermined the already shaky system by which Russia strove to protect her position in Europe; Moscow could no longer count on help from the West in resisting Hitler's expansion East. Furthermore, the strategic situation had been altered against Soviet interests. "There can be no doubt," writes Max Beloff, "that Czechoslovakia was the principal barrier to

181. Feiling, p. 392.
182. Thorne, p. 98.
183. Feiling, p. 393.
184. Thorne, p. 98.
185. George, p. 194.
186. Thorne, p. 100.

Germany's eastward expansion." [187] As Sumner Welles wrote in 1944, "The agreements of Munich confirmed the conviction of the Soviet government that the Western powers strove to keep Germany from the west only by turning her to the east." [188] After Munich, one prominent historian of the period has written, "Hitler was going East; every newspaper correspondent, every business house, every embassy and legation in Europe knew it and reported accordingly." [189] Of particular danger to Soviet Russia was the prospect of a Polish alliance with Germany, for "Germany could organize a serious campaign against the U.S.S.R. only from Polish territory." [190] Polish hostility to Russia was an unconcealed fact, the nonaggression agreement notwithstanding. During the Czech crisis, the Poles refused to allow the passage of Soviet troops, and threatened to attack Russia if Polish territory were violated. Now, with Hitler pressing his demands on Poland, the possibility of either a German-Polish alliance or a German invasion of Poland, which would not be resisted by the West, could not be excluded by Soviet policy makers. "Either way," writes Ulam, "Germany would effectively become a neighbor to the Soviet Union. . . . It became a vital objective of Soviet foreign policy that Poland should resist the German demands and, if attacked, should find allies in the West." [191]

Thus, in the period of the "Munich winter," Russia faced no imminent threat, but rather a situation in which the eventual confrontation between Russia and Nazi Germany had to be the major consideration in Soviet foreign policy. Stalin's paramount interest was to do everything in his power to avoid or delay such a confrontation. Ulam praises the "masterful coolness and strength of nerves" in Soviet diplomacy of this period, and although I disagree with his particular interpretation of Soviet reasoning, I believe that he is correct in his observation that

187. Beloff, p. 69.
188. Welles, p. 322.
189. Wheeler-Bennett, p. 326.
190. McSherry, p. 104.
191. Ulam, p. 261.

"now [the Soviets] tried hard to create an impression of Russian aloofness and self-confidence." [192] Stalin was sharper than the British appeasers; he realized, as he had always made clear in his efforts at collective security, that an essential element in a policy of resisting or containing Hitler was to present an image of strength and determination. To approach Hitler with offers to help him achieve his goals was to encourage him, for there was no more effective manner of convincing him of his opponent's weakness. There was no chance of collective security having its intended effect if Britain and France publicly shunned co-operation with Russia and privately displayed to Hitler their desperation for an agreement with him. Now Stalin would have to keep his options open, and work carefully to insure that he did not obstruct any conceivable alternative. After Munich, André Fontaine has suggested, Stalin decided to "put a second iron in the fire"—

> either an alliance with the West against Hitler or a Soviet rapprochement with Germany in order to give the U.S.S.R. time to get itself in better shape to resist the inevitable attack. It was preparing itself for either alternative, and it would choose between them at the appropriate time on the basis of what the two sides had to offer and of the state of the U.S.S.R.'s defenses.[193]

The essential qualification in the above-quoted passage is the specification that Stalin prepared for a possible Soviet-German rapprochement "in order to give the U.S.S.R. time to get itself in better shape to resist the inevitable attack." There is no evidence that Stalin at any time sought an understanding with Hitler as part of a broader scheme of recognizing a new European status quo and living in peace; Stalin doubtless recognized that long-range cooperation with Hitler was impossible. Furthermore, in the period of the Munich winter, there is no evidence that Stalin was actively pursuing a temporary rapprochement

192. Ibid., p. 259.
193. Fontaine, p. 100.

with Hitler. What he was doing was (1) keeping open his options for an agreement with Germany and (2) seeking a diplomatic edge vis-à-vis Britain and France by carefully exploiting economic negotiations with Germany.

By November of 1938, Germany's foreign trade and raw material situation was such that many efforts were made to expand trade, including overtures to England and Russia.[194] In December, the Director of the Economic Policy Department, Wiehl, began sounding out the Russians on resuming credit negotiations. The Soviet Ambassador in Berlin, Merekalov, was receptive to the idea and insisted that the negotiations take place in Moscow, as opposed to Berlin, where they had always occurred in the past. Wiehl was opposed to the idea for practical reasons, but recommended that the chairman of the German trade delegation, Schnurre, be sent to Moscow because Germany's need for raw materials and the credit agreement "is so great that it does not appear expedient to frustrate the negotiations in any way." However, the Germans did not miss the significance of this peculiar Soviet request (it would have been easier to hold the talks in Berlin): Wiehl wrote to State Secretary Weizacker, "The strong desire to have a German delegation come to Moscow can therefore only be interpreted in the sense that the Soviet Government would like to demonstrate to the outside world the value placed also by the Third Reich on the continuation of economic relations." News of Schnurre's pending visit was leaked to the press, and the Soviets did nothing to discourage or deny the reports. However, this publicity angered Ribbentrop, who canceled the visit on January 26.[195]

During approximately the same period, the British were engaged in a series of economic negotiations with Germany, but their intention was significantly different from that of the Soviets. While evidence is lacking that the Soviets regarded their credit negotiations with the Reich as anything other than a

194. McSherry, p. 115; Documents and Materials, 2: 162–63. (Hereinafter referred to as "Dirksen Papers.")
195. McSherry, pp. 115–18.

means of gaining valuable economic concessions, impressing and perhaps frightening the West, and keeping the door open to a possible future agreement with Hitler, the British approached their trade negotiations with the specific understanding that they were to pave the way for the farreaching agreement desired by Chamberlain. As relations between Britain and Germany cooled toward December, the German Ambassador in London, Dirksen, searched for a means of improving relations. Later he wrote, "I came to the conclusion that the *economic* way offered the best prospects." [196] It is doubless true, as his written recollections suggest, that Dirksen "came" to this conclusion under orders from Berlin, for at the time expanded export trade and raw materials were greatly needed by Germany. Dirksen continues:

> Consequently, in the middle of December, I began to lay increasing stress in my talks with influential Englishmen on the idea that the way to relieve the tension must be sought in the economic field: there were plenty of causes of political friction, but economic interests were common and they were capable of being developed; furthermore they at present held first place with us. It was therefore necessary and expedient to achieve calm and confidence by means of co-operation in the economic sphere; then we would see.[197]

By the end of January, the British demonstrated an eagerness to enter into significant economic negotiations with Germany. Plans were made for negotiations at Dusseldorf in late February between the central industrial federations of the two countries (the Federation of British Industries and the Reichsgruppe Industries). Chamberlain personally approved the negotiations and planned that in March the President of the Board of Trade, Oliver Stanley, should visit Berlin.[198] The British attached importance to the visit to Berlin of someone of such high standing as Stanley, and "trial ballons" were released by the British for a

196. Dirksen Papers, p. 162.
197. Ibid., pp. 162–63.
198. Feiling, p. 396.

visit to Britain by a German official of equal standing.[199] In February, with the conclusion of a coal agreement and completion of final arrangements for the Dusseldorf conference and Stanley's visit, Dirksen noted, "The atmosphere was unusually favorable and also had an alleviating effect on the political tension." [200] On February 19, Chamberlain made a diary entry that expressed his optimism in poetic terms and concluded, "All the information I get seems to point in the direction of peace." [201] Buoyed by his optimism, Chamberlain spoke with a group of journalists in March and told them that he hoped for much from Stanley's visit to Berlin and that "a disarmament conference might meet before the year's end." [202]

At the same time, the British sent the head of the economic office of the Foreign Office, Frank Ashton-Gwatken, to Berlin to sound out top German leaders on the prospects of political negotiations. In a conversation with Wiehl on February 20, Ashton-Gwatken said "Britain was of the opinion that economic agreement must be reached between the two countries this year in order to put an end to the armaments, race." Wiehl told his visitor that an arms limitations agreement was a political rather than economic matter and that he was not "the proper authority" for the discussion of political questions.[203] Later the same day, Ashton-Gwatken met with Foreign Minister Ribbentrop, who gave a cold reception to ideas for political rapprochement. Ashton-Gwatken told Ribbentrop that his ideas on how to improve trade between the two countries (ostensibly the purpose of his visit) "extended beyond the limits of economy into the sphere of politics"; he "suggested that the Foreign Minister should invite Sir Horace Wilson to Germany." Ribbentrop replied that such an invitation was not possible "until clearer relations existed between Germany and Britain." [204] Before leaving Ger-

199. Dirksen Papers, pp. 163–66.
200. Ibid., p. 165.
201. Feiling, p. 396.
202. Ibid.
203. DGFP, 4: 408.
204. Ibid., pp. 410–12.

many, Ashton-Gwatken met again with Wiehl, who realized that the suggestion of an invitation of Horace Wilson to Germany was the most important of the British "political feelers." At the conclusion of this last meeting, Wiehl was asked if it was not possible to reach "an agreement between the two governments to undertake no alteration in the status quo during the next three to four years. When I [Wiehl] asked whether by that he meant a political peace pact, he answered in the affirmative." [205]

In the next month Britain's plans for rapprochement with Germany received a rude shock when Hitler, with the help of Poland and Hungary, invaded the remainder of Czechoslovakia.

205. Ibid., pp. 419–20.

3

"As Ye Sow . . ."

Between March 13 and 17, 1939, Hitler embarked on the final dismemberment of Czechoslovakia. On March 15, German troops occupied the Czech provinces of Bohemia and Moravia, and Hitler, having arrived in Prague, proclaimed a German Protectorate over Czechoslovakia. The province of Slovakia declared its independence and the following day requested a protectorate from Germany. The Hungarians, with covert Polish aid, invaded the extreme eastern tip of Czechoslovakia, the Carpatho-Ukraine to which they had laid claim since Munich. Hitler reluctantly approved the Hungarian occupation.

The first response of the British and French was one of relief. In their view, Hitler had liquidated the ambiguous commitment they made to Central Europe at Munich.[1] On the evening of March 14, Halifax deplored violence but disclaimed on the part of his government "the desire to interfere unnecessarily in

1. Thorne, pp. 104–5; Taylor, p. 203.

matters with which other Governments may be more directly concerned." [2] The same day Henderson assured German State Secretary Weizacker that "German interests were paramount in the Czech area." [3] On March 15, the day Prague was invaded, the British Government expressed their relief. Halifax wrote his ambassador in Paris that "the only compensating advantage that I saw was that it had brought to a natural end the somewhat embarrassing commitment of a guarantee, in which we and the French had been involved." [4] In the House of Commons, Chamberlain asserted that the British guarantee to Czechoslovakia was no longer valid. He reasoned that since Slovakia had declared its independence, it "put an end by internal disruption to the State whose frontiers we had proposed to guarantee, and His Majesty's Government cannot accordingly hold themselves bound by this obligation." [5] Chancellor of the Exchequer Simon told the Commons that it was impossible to fulfill a guarantee of a state which had ceased to exist.[6]

British public reaction to the German move was of indignation. Chamberlain, who had since Munich been resisting pressure to broaden his Cabinet, realized that he would have to take a stronger stand if only to preserve his political position.[7] In a speech at Birmingham on March 17 Chamberlain defended the Munich settlement and criticized Hitler for having broken his word. He said that for every German aggression up to this point "there was something to be said, whether on account of racial affinity or of just claims too long resisted." Now, Chamberlain asked if Hitler's new move was not "a step in the direction of an attempt to dominate the world by force?" He warned that even though he believed war "to be a senseless and cruel thing," England could not be counted on to withhold "the utmost of its

2. DBFP, 4, No. 247.
3. DGFP, 4, No. 213.
4. DBFP, 4, No. 280.
5. Churchill, p. 343.
6. Taylor, p. 203.
7. Colvin, p. 187; Birkenhead, p. 432.

power in resisting such a challenge if it ever were made." [8]

The days after March 17 were ominous indeed. On March 17 the Rumanian Minister in London, Tilea, informed Halifax that Bucharest was alarmed at the threatening attitude of Herr Wohlthat, head of the German economic mission negotiating a new trade agreement with Rumania. Tilea feared that Wohlthat would offer an ultimatum forcing Rumania into economic sub-servience to Germany. In addition, there were indications that Hungary was preparing for an attack on Rumania. Between March 20 and 23, Ribbentrop forced the Lithuanians to turn the port of Memel over to the Germans.

British policy in this period is difficult to assess. It is often asserted that the appeasement policy was laid to rest on March 17. No doubt, the German occupation of Czechoslovakia changed British policy. The essential question is, How? On March 15 Chamberlain expressed his bitterness at the German move, but pleaded, "Do not let us on that account be deflected from our course." [9] Indeed, there is no evidence that the *basic aims* of British policy changed after March 15; what underwent a radical change was the way in which those aims were pursued. Chamberlain still wanted peace, but he could no longer count on direct dealings or normal diplomacy with Hitler. When the Cabinet met on March 18, Chamberlain stated that "he had now come definitely to the conclusion that Herr Hitler's attitude made it impossible to continue to negotiate on the old basis with the Nazi regime. This did not mean that negotiations with the German people were impossible." He outlined the next step as being "to ascertain what friends we have who will join us in resisting aggression." The Cabinet agreed that in the event of war, it was vital that Germany be compelled to fight on two fronts. The key to the problem, thought Chamberlain, was Poland.[10] "As soon as I had time to think," Chamberlain wrote

8. Feiling, p. 400.
9. Churchill, p. 343.
10. Colvin, pp. 188–89.

on March 19, "I saw that it was impossible to deal with Hitler after he had thrown all his assurances to the winds." [11] In the same diary entry, he wrote, "As always, I want to gain time, for I never accept the view that war is inevitable."

The two immediate needs facing British policy makers after March 15 were these: (1) to adopt a policy flexible enough to deter war—yet strong enough to avoid alienating public opinion in England, and (2) to assure that, in the event Hitler decided to make war, he would be tied up in the east. A. J. P. Taylor has described Britain's policy in light of these two central needs. To appease the British public, the "emphasis," not the "direction" of policy was changed: "Previously the British government often warned Hitler in private, while pursuing appeasement in public. Now they warned him publicly and went on with appeasement in private." [12] Sir Samuel Hoare wrote that "the lesson of Prague was not that further efforts for peace were futile, but rather that, without greater force behind them, negotiations and agreements with Hitler were of no permanent value." [13] According to Taylor,

> A general settlement with Hitler remained the British object; and they put obstacles in his way so that he would incline more readily to agreement. The British ministers did not fear defeat in war, though they naturally dreaded war for its own sake. . . . What they feared, with some justification, was that Hitler would count on their standing aside. They therefore took steps to demonstrate that they might not do so. Compulsory military service of a limited kind was introduced at the end of April; guarantees were distributed to supposedly threatened states. *These steps were not practical, effective preparations for a general war: they were warnings, designed to avoid such a war.*[14]

I would agree with Taylor in every respect except one; he underrates the British fear of war. Although their major concern was

11. Feiling, p. 401.
12. Taylor, pp. 205–6.
13. Sir Samuel Hoare, *Nine Troubled Years* (London: Collins, 1954), p. 377.
14. Taylor, pp. 205–6. Emphasis added.

not *defeat* in war, they were quite fearful of the sacrifices they might have to make in a *long* war, and the possible consequences both at home and abroad. As early as March 20, 1938, Chamberlain wrote that he would not think of going to war with Germany "unless we had a reasonable prospect of being able to beat her to her knees *in a reasonable time*." [15]

The British and the French suffered the anxiety of not knowing where Hitler would strike next. "We have so many open doors in front of us," said one of Goebbels's lieutenants to Coulondre on March 18, "so many possibilities, that we don't know which way to turn." [16] What the British Cabinet wanted to avoid most was a turn to the West by Hitler. Their policy was therefore to deter Hitler from making war by what they considered an adequate show of force; should this fail to deter Hitler, it was vital that he attack in the East and that he be sufficiently tied up there that he could not contemplate an attack in the West. Thus, the primary concern of the British and the French after the occupation of Prague was to erect a "peace front" in Eastern Europe to guarantee that Hitlerian aggression in that area would be resisted. While there is no firm evidence that either government desired to turn Hitler loose on Soviet Russia specifically, the concern to keep Hitler occupied in the East inevitably had a profound effect on relations with Russia.

In order to understand Britain's "Peace Front" policy, one must examine British anxieties about Hitler in the period of the Munich winter. In spite of Chamberlain's optimism in mid-February that peace was at hand, the British had been receiving intelligence that Hitler was planning further aggression. In the immediate aftermath of Munich there were persuasive signs that Germany was laying the foundation for an attack on the Russian Ukraine.

During the Munich crisis, Hungary pressed her claims against Ruthenia, a Ukrainian province located at the extreme eastern tip of Czechoslovakia. Hungary received strong support from

15. Feiling, p. 348.
16. Thorne, p. 113.

Poland's Foreign Minister Beck, who wished to bring about a common Polish-Hungarian frontier. The Czechs, with German encouragement, resisted Hungary's claims on Ruthenia (later called the Carpatho-Ukraine). The British understood why Hitler would not want to see Ruthenia absorbed by Hungary. As Oliver Harvey wrote in his diary on October 22, 1938:

> Germany is believed to be opposed to the Beck plan as she is anxious to keep open the Ruthenian corridor towards the Ukraine for future eventualities. . . . Czechoslovakia from having been a dagger pointed to the heart of Germany is now rapidly being organized as a dagger into Russian vitals.[17]

With German support and encouragement after Munich, Ruthenia "rapidly became the much publicized centre of the idea of a 'Great Ukraine.'" The local Government, whose first action upon gaining autonomy on October 11, 1938, was to suppress the Communist Party, "talked more or less openly of the coming creation of a Great Ukraine and of the liberation of their kinsmen from the yoke of Poland and Russia."[18] The British recognized that Hitler in his manipulation of Ukrainian nationalism was laying the foundation for an attack on Poland or Russia. On December 25 Harvey wrote that "the whole question is whether Hitler is going East to the Ukraine, or whether before going East he feels he must deal with the West first."[19] When Chamberlain met with Mussolini on January 11, he immediately asked the Italian leader if he could give him any reassurance about the menacing German activities, which seemed to indicate Hitler's intention to attack the Polish or Russian Ukraine and which had the whole of Europe in a state of nervous anticipation. Mussolini denied that Hitler had any aggressive intentions, but his explanations did not satisfy Chamberlain or Halifax.[20] To-

17. Harvey, p. 215.
18. Beloff, p. 215.
19. Harvey, p. 232.
20. Malcolm Muggeridge, ed. *Ciano's Diplomatic Papers* (London: Odhams Press Ltd., 1948), pp. 263–64; DBFP, 3: 524–25; Birkenhead, pp. 429–30; Halifax, p. 202.

ward the end of January, there were indications from the Soviet-German trade talks that relations in that quarter were improving. On February 1 Alexander Cadogan wrote in his minutes:

> If we may believe that the Germans have found that their project for acquiring a dominating position in the Ukraine was not so realisable as they had thought, it may well be that they have turned their minds to obtaining a form of economic cooperation with, if not domination of, the Soviet. . . . It seems to me that we shall have to watch very carefully the development of any tendency towards a rapprochement between Germany and the Soviet.[21]

A British reporter publicly warned at this time that "a dangerous day for Britain and France will come should the Nazis decide that the dream of colonizing the Ukraine . . . is a dream that can never become a reality." [22]

British anxiety was so great by the end of January 1939 that an appeal was sent to Washington under Halifax's signature. In a lengthy letter, the British Foreign Office summarized their latest disturbing intelligence:

> As early as November there were indications which gradually became more definite that Hitler was planning a further foreign adventure for the spring of 1939. At first it appeared —and this was confirmed by persons in Hitler's entourage— that he was thinking of expansion in the east and in December the prospect of establishing an independent Ukraine under German vassalage was freely spoken of in Germany.
> Since then reports indicate that Hitler . . . is considering an attack on the Western Powers as a preliminary to subsequent action in the east.[23]

Halifax presented this information to the Cabinet in a meeting on January 25. He concluded, "We have very definite indications that Herr Hitler may be contemplating an attack on the West

21. DBFP, 4: 70–71.
22. Beloff, p. 217.
23. FRUS (1939), 1: 2–6.

during the coming spring." Halifax was careful to point out, respecting Chamberlain's belief that Hitler did not wish to make war, that "we have no proof that the Führer has definitely committed himself to such action." The Foreign Secretary made one further observation, which provides the key to Britain's foreign policy up to the outbreak of World War II:

> All that can be said with practical certainty is that an "explosion" of Germany is likely to come in the comparatively near future and that it is necessary for us to take immediate measures to guard against the possibility of it being directed against us.[24]

D. F. Fleming has suggested that the German consent to the Hungarian annexation of the Carpatho-Ukraine on March 16, 1939, sounded "an alarm bell" in London that Hitler "was not going to tangle with Russia" and might "clean up the West first." [25] Certainly the German action signaled an end to any immediate plans to invade the Russian Ukraine.[26] However, it was during the two months prior to the March aggressions that the British Cabinet began to suffer the anxiety that Hitler might deal with the West before turning east. It is vital to recognize that it was during this period that the Cabinet reached the understanding, which was to become policy after March 15, that in order to save Britain and British interests in the West, Hitler's fury must be absorbed in the east.

Immediately after the occupation of Czechoslovakia, the most threatened nation seemed to be Rumania, and Britain frantically searched for a policy with the view of deterring Hitler from aggression against Rumania. The British idea was to have each of Rumania's neighbors issue a guarantee against unprovoked aggression. Toward this end, Halifax, on March 18, asked Soviet Ambassador Maisky what his government would do in the event of an unprovoked attack on Rumania.[27] The Soviet

24. Colvin, p. 180.
25. Fleming, p. 86.
26. Ulam, p. 264.
27. Namier, pp. 82–83.

response, delivered the next day, proposed a conference to be convened immediately at Bucharest, at which the powers most directly concerned—Britain, France, Russia, Poland, Rumania, and Turkey—would consider the question of German aggression.[28] Halifax rejected this proposal as "premature." The same day Chamberlain wrote in his diary about a "pretty bold and startling" plan that he had devised and intended to put to the Cabinet the following day. The plan was designed to buy time, and Chamberlain was confident that "it won't bring us to an acute crisis." [29] On the evening of March 20 this plan went into effect. A proposal was sent to Moscow, Warsaw, and Paris for a joint declaration that consultations would be held to decide on the steps necessary to resist "a threat to the political independence of any European State." [30] Litvinov replied on March 23 that Moscow was ready to sign the agreement as soon as France and Poland had promised to do so.[31]

The Poles threatened to wreck the British plan because they refused to sign any agreement with Russia. Foreign Minister Beck had long tried to balance his country between Russia and Germany, and now he argued to the British that Poland would provoke an attack by Germany if it entered into such an agreement with Russia. Bonnet and Halifax met in London on March 21 and 22 to discuss the proposed four-power declaration, and their conversation was quite frank and revealing. The greatest concern of the Foreign Ministers was that Eastern Europe might offer no resistance to an attack by Hitler. Obviously, if that were the case, Hitler could consolidate his position in Central and Eastern Europe in no time and strike in the West.[32] Thus, Halifax and Bonnet spoke strongly of the need to force Poland to announce her determination to resist aggression. "It was absolutely essential to get Poland in," Bonnet said. "Russian help

28. Ibid.
29. Feiling, p. 401.
30. DBFP, 4, No. 446.
31. Thorne, p. 117.
32. The Foreign Office had supported this theory. See DBFP, 4, Appendix IV.

would be effective only if Poland were collaborating. . . . The strongest pressure must therefore be brought to bear upon Poland." The official record of the meeting quotes Halifax as "entirely of M. Bonnet's opinion." To assure Poland's cooperation, Halifax said, he recognized the "need for using very plain language to the Polish Government." Bonnet said "it was desirable, therefore, to go to the utmost limit, even to the extent of threats, to bring Poland in." Bonnet was quite candid: if no East European country offered resistance to aggression by Hitler, "France would be in a bad position. It was therefore necessary that the countries most interested should pronounce themselves, and the Poles were certainly interested. . . ." [33] At another meeting of the Foreign Ministers attended by Chamberlain, Halifax made a suggestion with which Bonnet was in agreement:

> In order to persuade Poland to commit herself to support Rumania, Great Britain and France would have to give Poland a private understanding that, if Poland came in, they would both come in also. Having reached this understanding with Poland, it might be suggested to both Poland and Rumania that they should not raise any objection to our doing our best, both in their interest and in our own, to secure Soviet participation. [34]

At this point, the British had more faith in a Polish-Rumanian alliance than in any pact with Russia to resist German aggression. Apparently accepting Beck's delusions about Poland's strength and ignoring their own intelligence reports describing Poland's unpreparedness for war, the British Cabinet felt, according to Sir Samuel Hoare, that "Poland was a more valuable ally than Russia." [35] On March 24 Halifax told Kennedy that, based on his information, the most that could be expected from Russia would be "some ammunition to Poland in the event of

33. Ibid., pp. 422–27.
34. Ibid., pp. 457–63.
35. Hoare, p. 344.

trouble," and that Poland was of more value as an ally of Rumania than Russia.[36] On March 26, Chamberlain wrote in his diary, "I must confess to the most profound distrust of Russia. I have no belief whatever in her ability to maintain an effective offensive, even if she wanted to. And I distrust her motives." [37] In early April when Beck told him "he was very anxious not to be tied up with Russia," Chamberlain wrote, "I confess I very much agree with him, for I regard Russia as a very unreliable friend." [38]

On March 23, Beck sent a proposal to London that rejected the four power declaration and asked if the British would not consider immediately concluding with Poland "a bilateral agreement in the spirit of the proposed declaration." [39] After this proposal was made, the Poles refused Hitler's demands with regard to Danzig, and storm signals went out that Poland might soon be the next victim of Nazi aggression. Regardless of the veracity of these signals, they apparently produced their effect on Chamberlain, who, on March 30, personally drafted a temporary unilateral guarantee to Poland pending further negotiations. The guarantee was communicated through the British Ambassador in Poland and Beck accepted it immediately.[40] The following day, Chamberlain announced the terms of the guarantee before the House of Commons:

> In the event of any action which already threatened Polish independence, and which the Polish Government accordingly considered it vital to resist with national forces, His Majesty's Government would feel themselves bound at once to lend the Polish Government all support in their power. . . . I may add that the French Government have authorized me to make it plain that they stand in the same position as does His Majesty's Government.[41]

36. New York Times Magazine, July 18, 1943; Namier, p. 93.
37. Feiling, p. 403.
38. Ibid., p. 408.
39. Namier, p. 94.
40. DBFP, 4, No. 568.
41. Wheeler-Bennett, p. 374.

By any rational standards, Britain would not have made such a guarantee unless she thoroughly expected that Hitler would not attack Poland in the foreseeable future. The British sensed a bad situation and hoped this guarantee would steady things; the Cabinet was not so desperate as to leave the decision for war or peace "in the hands of a State ruled by an incompetent and purblind oligarchy who preferred government by junta rather than by parliament." [42] Beck boasted to Kennedy that he was "more than happy to have England's support given in the way that it was, i.e., that Poland is the one to determine when England is to come to her rescue." [43] But Beck firmly believed that Hitler would not dare to go to war over Danzig and he doubtless influenced the British Cabinet, to whom he was still lying about German diplomatic pressure on the Poles.[44]

When the guarantee to Poland was debated in Parliament on April 3, Lloyd George spoke for a disapproving minority. "I cannot understand why," he said, "before committing ourselves to this tremendous enterprise, we did not secure the adhesion of Russia." He asked how Britain could possibly make good on her pledge without Russia. "If war occurred tomorrow, you (or France) could not send a single battalion to Poland." Russia alone could reach the Poles. George pointed out the correct policy:

> If Russia has not been brought into this matter because of certain feelings the Poles have that they do not want the Russians there, it is for us to declare the conditions, and unless they are prepared to accept the only conditions under which we can successfully help them, the responsibility must be theirs.[45]

The method suggested by George was not at all unacceptable to the British Cabinet; in the Anglo-French conversations of March 21 and 22, Halifax and Chamberlain had agreed to use

42. Ibid., p. 375.
43. FRUS (1939), 1: 112–13.
44. Thorne, pp. 27–28; Namier, p. 149.
45. Namier, pp. 109–10.

all forms of pressure to assure Polish cooperation with British aims, and Halifax himself had proposed threatening the Poles with abandonment if they refused Russian aid. It was the *object* of George's suggestion that was so distasteful to the British leaders and that Chamberlain and Halifax were allowing the Poles to thwart—an agreement with Russia. In a meeting with Beck on April 5, Halifax "pressed Beck as to whether he would not want tanks, airplanes and ammunition, at least, from Russia if Poland were attacked, and, even with that as bait, Beck said no." [46] If the British found Beck's refusal unacceptable, they would have put the pressure on him; they did not because, as Chamberlain admitted, they agreed with Beck.[47] Although Beck would not hear of any closer ties between his country and Russia beyond their trading agreement, he let the British know that he would remain neutral should Britain desire closer cooperation with Russia in regard to guaranteeing Eastern Europe. While this might have served the interests of British foreign policy, it did little to fulfill the great needs of Soviet security.

What was Soviet policy after March 15? By all indications, Stalin became even more concerned about Soviet security, although he continued to maintain his composure. It was in his interest to encourage the countries along his Western border to resist Hitler, but with Hungary already on Hitler's side and Poland, Rumania, and Finland inclining toward Hitler and hostile to political cooperation with Russia, this was not a realistic prospect, and Stalin could not base his foreign policy on so undependable a set of circumstances. As already mentioned, he proposed to the British on March 19 a conference of concerned nations, a proposal that Halifax rejected. Around March 15 Maisky gave an unofficial assurance to the Rumanian Ambassador that Russia would make all possible aid available to Rumania in the event of an attack by either Germany or Hungary.[48] On March 28 Litvinov delivered identical notes to the

46. FRUS (1939), 1: 113–14.
47. Feiling, p. 408.
48. DBFP, 4: 448–50.

Latvian and Estonian Ministers in Moscow. These notes stipulated that *any* form of infringement on the independence and
sovereignty of either state by a third state "would be recognized
by the Soviet Government as insufferable":

> This declaration is made . . . with the purpose of enhancing
> in [each nation] a feeling of security and confidence in the
> readiness of the Soviet Union to prove with deeds, in case of
> need, its interest in preserving in its entirety for [each nation]
> its sovereign existence as a state and its political and economic
> independence, as well as confidence in the inability of the
> Soviet Union to remain an idle bystander of open or masked
> attempts to destroy this sovereignty and independence.[49]

Thus, in the case of these two small nations, Russia preserved
her freedom of action and made a matter of record her determination to intervene under circumstances *that she alone would
define*. Obviously, Stalin was not in a position to dictate such
terms to Poland. However, he was quite anxious that the British
guarantee of Poland be as strong as possible and that Moscow's
approval of the pledge be publicly announced. Ulam has noted
Halifax's "incredible blindness" in a conversation with Maisky
on March 31 concerning the British pledge to Poland. Maisky,
who had previously insisted on consulting with his government
on matters of much less importance than this, gave his immediate
approval to a declaration by Chamberlain that Moscow understood and appreciated the principles on which the British
government acted. Writes Ulam: "To a man more perceptive
than Lord Halifax, it would have been clear that Maisky must
have been briefed for precisely such an occasion and that be-
neath his nonchalant and amiable behavior there was an obvious
anxiety that the declaration be made and that it not be delayed
by one day, one hour." [50]

With regard to a possible rapprochement with Hitler, there
is no reason to believe that during the first half of 1939 such an

49. McSherry, p. 124.
50. Ulam, pp. 266-67; DBFP, 4: 557.

idea was anything more for Stalin than an option he could not afford to foreclose. Western observers had little difficulty in discerning that an agreement with Hitler would have to remain one of Stalin's options, although Halifax and Chamberlain were confident that such a combination could never come about. As early as January 18, 1939, the U.S. Ambassador in Moscow, Joseph Davies, wrote that "the Chamberlain policy of throwing Italy, Poland and Hungary into the arms of Hitler may be completed by so disgusting the Soviets that it will drive Russia into an economic agreement and an ideological truce with Hitler." [51] On April 13, the British Ambassador in Moscow, William Seeds, wrote to Halifax of the danger that in the event of war in the Balkans, Hitler might reach an agreement with Stalin.[52] Stalin's speech of March 10 has often been interpreted as his first gesture toward Hitler. I agree with the historian of the period who has written that "no evidence supports such an idea." [53] Furthermore, as Ulam has pointed out, "On March 10 nothing indicated that a bargain with Hitler was a real possibility. Stalin had nothing to sell." [54]

Although Stalin doubtless welcomed the British commitment to Poland and later to Rumania (on April 13), he could not help but regard the guarantee with a well-justified skepticism. The British had urged the French to break their treaty with Czechoslovakia and then weaseled out of an ambiguous guarantee of Czechoslovakia's post-Munich borders. Indeed, how could anyone not regard the new pledges with skepticism when the British Government promised action that it had heretofore refused to take and now left the decision in the hands of another country? For Stalin in particular there was a special reason to be skeptical. The Soviet Union, the one nation in a position to render effective aid to Poland in the event of an attack, had not been consulted by the British in connection with this guarantee;

51. Joseph Davies, *Mission to Moscow* (New York: Pocket Books Inc., 1943), p. 379.
52. DBFP, 5:104.
53. McSherry, p. 119.
54. Ulam, p. 264.

indeed, Maisky was not informed of the guarantee until after the Poles had accepted it.[55] On April 1, the day after Chamberlain announced the guarantee, Litvinov complained to Seeds that the Soviets were in the dark as to what the British were planning. He probed Seeds to discover the validity of the British commitment; as Seeds reported, Litvinov "expressed doubts whether we could regard attack on Danzig or Corridor as threatening Poland's independence." [56] On April 14, the day after the British guaranteed Rumania, Maisky met with Halifax to announce his government's readiness to aid Rumania and "to learn the views of His Majesty's Government as to the best methods by which such assistance could be given and as to the part the various Powers concerned could play in helping Rumania." [57]

The response to Maisky's request made it clear that the British did not expect war and did not desire tangible Soviet assistance beyond a declaration to deter Hitler. Halifax proposed a unilateral Soviet declaration "that in the event of any act of aggression against any European neighbor of the Soviet Union which was resisted by the country concerned, the assistance of the Soviet Government would be available, if desired, and would be afforded in such a manner as would be found most convenient." In his instructions to Seeds, Halifax noted that such a statement would have a "steadying effect on the international situation." [58] There was not the slightest chance that Russia would make such a declaration. It would limit her freedom of action by making her aid dependent on the wishes of smaller nations; a major power whose vital interests were at stake simply could not adopt a policy based on the two premises of the British proposal: (1) that the countries involved would resist pressure from Hitler and, (2) if they did, that they would "desire" help from Russia. Furthermore, as Chamberlain explained to the House of Commons, the proposed Soviet guarantee was to apply only "in the event of Great Britain and France being in-

55. Namier, p. 111.
56. DBFP, 4: 574–75.
57. Ibid., 5: 201–2.
58. Ibid., p. 206.

volved in hostilities in discharge of their own obligations." [59]
Cadogan frankly admitted to the Cabinet on April 19 that the
request for a unilateral Soviet declaration had been made "in
order to placate our left wing in England, rather than to obtain
any solid military advantage." [60]

When Seeds presented the proposal to Litvinov on April 16,
the latter replied that it was not a response to Maisky's inquiry.
Litvinov repeated Russia's readiness "in principle" to aid Rumania, but asked again "how far Great Britain and other countries were prepared to go when it came to the point." The
Foreign Commisar was blunt: "How do we know that Great
Britain will declare war in case of armed aggression?" Moreover,
as Seeds recognized, Litvinov feared that one of Britain's objectives might be to get the Soviet Union committed in a way
by which Britain and France could unload the burden of their
commitments to fight onto Russia, or, as Seeds put it, that
Russia was being "maneuvered into holding the baby." [61]

As of April 1939, it is reasonably certain that the primary
purpose of the proposed Soviet declaration, from the British
point of view, was to produce a deterring effect on Hitler.
Nevertheless, the British were asking the Russians to make a
specific commitment in Eastern Europe, a commitment that
would enable the British and French to shift the burden of
fighting onto the Soviet Union in the event of war. They asked
Russia to make this commitment on a unilateral basis, without
any provision for reciprocity, and on conditions that would allow
her policy to be dictated by states hostile toward her. One historian has concisely described the British position: "They wanted
to preserve a situation, not to change it. This meant that they
were asking of the Soviet Union the promise of an enormous
effort, quite notably involving a war against Germany, in return
for nothing." [62] It was a unique blindness and prejudice that
enabled the British and the French to attempt to deal with the

59. Namier, pp. 151–52.
60. Colvin, p. 200.
61. DBFP, 5: 221–24.
62. Laurence Lafore, *The End of Glory* (Philadephia; J. B.
Lippincott Co., 1970), p. 254.

Soviet Union on such a basis. Stalin was willing to commit himself in Eastern Europe, but only on his terms and in a manner that would permit him the freedom of action necessary to protect Russia's vital interests in all possible contingencies. In diplomatic terms, Stalin was offering to help Britain and France in commitments they had made entirely on their own, but he was asking a price for his help. There was nothing sinister in Stalin's position, and nothing less could have been expected of any other leader in defense of his country. A. J. P. Taylor has stated the issue well. He believes that the Russians were reluctant to act; "but if they acted," he writes, "particularly if they went to war—it would not be to preserve the treaty settlements of Brest–Litovsk and Riga. They would return to world affairs only as a Great Power, the equal of Great Britain and paramount in Eastern Europe." [63] Arnold Toynbee stated the obvious when he wrote that "the geographical situation of the various states concerned meant, as the Russians perceived, that they [the Russians] would have to bear the brunt of giving direct and immediate help to any Eastern European state that might be the victim of aggression." [64] Another prominent historian of the period, L. B. Namier, has also pointed out that "the supposition that in case of war [Russia] would have had to bear the main burden was not unreasonable." Stalin's price for agreeing to bear this burden was that Russia should "hold the principal place in Eastern Europe, to which her size and power entitled her." [65]

Perhaps as of early 1938 Stalin might have been more inclined to issue a declaration of the type desired by Britain. It was then conceivable that such a declaration would have helped contain Hitler, if backed by adequate force and a determination to use it. But in April 1939, after Hitler's war machine had gained precious time to expand and develop, after the valuable Skoda munitions factories of Czechoslovakia had fallen

63. Taylor, p. 233.
64. Arnold Toynbee, ed., *The Eve of War 1939* (London: Royal Institute for the Study of International Affairs, 1958), p. 441.
65. Namier, p. xv.

into German hands, and as the countries of the *cordon sanitaire* threatened to fall victim to open or covert Nazi aggression, Stalin's attitude was different. Now, as Taylor points out, the Russians "were not concerned to sustain Poland or to provide some moral display against Hitler. They wished to secure precise and rigid military backing from the Western powers in case Hitler attacked Russia—either through Poland or more directly." [66] This included the Baltic states, through which Hitler could conceivably have launched an attack on the vulnerable Leningrad. Previously, the Soviets had taken steps to assure their freedom to take action in Latvia and Estonia if Stalin deemed it necessary. Soviet efforts to prevent the possibility that Hitler might use Finnish territory to invade the U.S.S.R. were unsuccessful because of the hostile attitude of the Finnish Government.[67]

With all of these considerations in mind, the Soviets on April 17 put forth to Britain and France a comprehensive proposal. This proposal initiated a series of negotiations to which the remainder of this chapter is devoted. In their proposal, the Soviets were forthright and candid; in effect, Stalin said to London and Paris, "We can help each other, but the circumstances are such that I must inevitably contribute more in the event of war than either of you could; here is what I am asking in return for my help." The significant elements of the Soviet proposal are these:

1. England, France and U.S.S.R. to conclude with one another an agreement for a period of five to ten years by which they would oblige themselves to render mutually forthwith all manner of assistance, including that of a military nature, in case of aggression in Europe against any one of the contracting Powers.

2. England, France and U.S.S.R. to undertake to render all manner of assistance, including that of a military nature, to Eastern European States situated between Baltic and Black Seas and bordering on U.S.S.R., in case of aggression against these States.

66. Taylor, p. 235.
67. Fontaine, pp. 107–8.

3. England, France and U.S.S.R. to undertake to discuss and to settle within shortest period of time extent and forms of military assistance to be rendered by each of these States in fulfillment of paragraphs 1 and 2. . . .

7. An agreement on the above lines to be signed simultaneously with terms of convention which has been described above under paragraph 3.[68]

From the point of view of Soviet needs and experience, these proposals were entirely reasonable. The revised British guarantee to Poland of April 6 and the guarantees to Rumania and Greece were bilateral and reciprocal; Britain and France promised to aid the guaranteed states in the event of an attack on them and those states in return promised to aid Britain and France should Hitler strike in the West. Yet, Britain and France asked Russia to promise her help with no provision for reciprocal aid should Russia be attacked. With their proposal, the Soviets merely asked for what the smaller powers of Eastern Europe had been readily granted: commitments for "mutual . . . assistance" from Britain and France. Furthermore, a commitment to aid only Poland and Rumania at their request, such as the British wanted from the Soviets, could not possibly serve the far greater needs of Soviet security. As Taylor points out, "There was no British commitment towards the Baltic States; here was the loophole for a German attack on Soviet Russia, while the Western Powers remained neutral." [69] Thus, said the Soviets in their proposal, if the British and the French wanted Russian help, they would have to agree to guarantee all states "bordering on the U.S.S.R." against aggression, without any provision that such aid be rendered only if requested by the particular state. Stalin specifically avoided any language prohibiting a signatory from rendering aid independently of the other two; in other words, aid could be given on an individual basis by England, France, or the U.S.S.R., although each would be committed to make some contribution. The provision that a military convention setting forth the "extent

68. DBFP, 5, No. 201.
69. Taylor, p. 236.

and forms of military assistance to be rendered by each of these States in fulfillment of " the agreement be signed simultaneously with the agreement itself was well justified after the experience of the Franco-Soviet and Czech-Soviet treaties. France had repeatedly refused to enter into staff talks to settle the military issues involved in the Soviet commitments to Czechoslovakia under these treaties; thus, when Czechoslovakia was threatened, the treaties proved meaningless. In principle, the French agreed with this aspect of the new Soviet proposal. In discussing the commitment to Poland with Halifax on March 21, 1939, Bonnet cited the failure of France to obtain permission from Poland or Rumania for the passage of Soviet troops to Czechoslovakia in 1938. "For this kind of reason," Bonnet said, "it was necessary for each party to say exactly what it would do—what material it would send; how many guns; how many aircraft; what number of troops. All these questions must be cleared up." [70]

Throughout the negotiations, which lasted until the signing of the Nazi-Soviet pact at the end of August 1939, the Russians were consistent in insisting on the fulfillment of these three basic terms: a reciprocal agreement to protect the U.S.S.R. from attack, a flexible guarantee for all states bordering on Russia in Europe, and a specific military convention to accompany the political agreement. Many critics and historians have accused the Russians of raising or changing their demands as the negotiations proceeded. This is inaccurate. Where the Russians revised any of their proposals, it was in response to a substantive change insisted upon by Britain and did not alter the basic Russian position. Although the Russians have been accused of insincerity and bad faith in these negotiations, I will argue and demonstrate that on the basis of their position throughout the negotiations the Russians cannot be reproached; there is nothing to indicate that, until the last minute, when Hitler offered an immediate and highly appealing settlement to Stalin, the Russians were not ready and willing to sign an agreement with

70. DBFP, 4: 422–27.

Britain and France if the latter two accepted the three terms deemed essential by Stalin.

Most accusations of Stalin's bad faith have been based on the fact that, at the same time he was negotiating with the British and French for an alliance against Hitler, he was sending feelers to the German government for a general political settlement. Rather than indicating Stalin's bad faith, these tentative gestures toward Germany merely underscore Stalin's realism and pragmatism. He had every reason to believe that he could not count on the British or the French to provide the assurances necessary for a Soviet commitment in Eastern Europe; with this in mind he had to keep open the option of a time-buying agreement with Hitler. (It should also be pointed out, as I will later document, that during the negotiations the British also continued to put out political feelers toward Germany.) On April 17, the day the Soviets made their proposal to Britain and France, the Russian Ambassador in Berlin called upon State Secretary Weizsacker and hinted that there were grounds to hope for improved relations "on a normal footing" between Germany and Russia.[71] The Germans did not respond to this feeler and in the following weeks, "both parties continued to make very cautious and tentative feelers" related to economic negotiations.[72] On May 20, the German Ambassador in Moscow, Schulenburg, was given orders to inform Molotov, the new Foreign Minister, that Berlin was ready to resume the economic negotiations suspended in February at the cancellation of Schnurre's visit. Molotov replied that the negotiations could resume only when the necessary "political basis" had been established. Despite Schulenburg's probing, Molotov would not elaborate on the nature of the "political basis" he had in mind.[73] Throughout, it was the Germans who took the initiatives that led to the Nazi-Soviet pact; the Russians merely indicated their willingness to talk, and even then they were strongly influenced by British moves, which signaled to

71. Ulam, p. 271.
72. McSherry, p. 148.
73. Ibid., p. 151.

Stalin that the negotiations for an alliance against Hitler would not succeed.

At first, the British had absolutely no intention of forming an alliance with Soviet Russia. In a letter to Ambassador Phipps of April 21, Halifax outlined British policy toward the Soviet proposal in almost Machiavellian terms. The British Foreign Secretary virtually admitted that Britain needed the Poles to absorb Hitler's fury. He revealed no concern for an effective means of saving Poland; privately the Cabinet Ministers admitted to each other that Britain neither could nor *would* do anything to save Poland.[74] His only concern was that the Polish Government have the determination to fight (by this time he knew that it did not have the means[75]):

> It is undesirable to do anything to disturb Polish confidence at the present time and it is important that Polish self-reliance should be maintained. To enter into an arrangement with the Soviet Government at this stage by which Soviet assistance would be afforded, whether Poland likes it or not, would have a most disturbing influence in Warsaw which is nearest to the danger, and might jeopardise the success already achieved by His Majesty's Government and the French Government in rallying Poland to the common cause.[76]

Halifax did not mean by this that the British did not desire Russian aid: "On the contrary they are conscious that the support that might be afforded by the Soviet Government to the small East European countries might be of the utmost value in case of war." However, the Governments of these small countries did not wish to be publicly associated with a guarantee by Russia. A month earlier Halifax had told Oliver Harvey that for fear of alienating Poland and Italy "we cannot have Russia in the forefront of the picture, although both for internal reasons and because of her ultimate military value, if only as our arsenal, we

74. Sidney Aster, *1939: The Making of the Second World War* (New York: Simon and Schuster, 1973).
75. DBFP, 5: 38–44.
76. Ibid., p. 268.

must keep her with us." [77] Halifax elaborated on this problem in his letter of April 21:

> It is to meet this difficulty that His Majesty's Government have proposed that the Soviet Government should of their own volition make a declaration which would steady the situation by showing the willingness of the Soviet Government to collaborate and which at the same time would not disturb the possible beneficiaries of Soviet assistance by requiring them to accede to any arrangement to which the Soviet government was a party. By this proposal the Soviet Government would place their help . . . at the disposal of States victims of aggression and themselves determined to resist, who wished to take advantage of it.

A week later Halifax wrote Phipps that it is "of such great importance . . . to shape any arrangement as to make it clear that Soviet assistance should be given only if desired and in the most convenient form." [78] Halifax readily admitted that he wanted the Soviet declaration only for the purpose of "steadying the situation." Furthermore, his proposal would have laid the basis for a German attack on the Soviet Union in which every European could remain neutral or even anti-Soviet. In the very possible event that Hitler took over Poland and Rumania, with or without resistance, he would be in a position to launch a massive invasion of Soviet Russia and Britain would be bound by no commitments to help.

Of particular interest is a conversation between Chamberlain and Kennedy on April 17, immediately before the Russian proposal was delivered to the British. According to Kennedy, Chamberlain said that "he feels he can make a deal with Russia at any time now, but is delaying until he definitely gets the Balkan situation straightened away, because it had been intimated to him that to bring Russia in before the Balkan deals are all completed might cause trouble." [79] Although this account is not without ambiguity, it does provide evidence that Chamber-

77. Harvey, p. 268.
78. Ibid., p. 358.
79. FRUS (1939), 1: 139–40.

lain was deliberately procrastinating about reaching an agreement with Russia until the British position in the Balkans could
be improved, that is, until Britain was in a better position to
block any move by Russia for predominance in that region.

Against this background, it is not surprising that a Cabinet
meeting of April 25 resulted in a decision to reject the Soviet
proposal and play for time. Arguments were exchanged on the
military value of Russia as an ally. Chamberlain expressed the
view, which he said was shared by the Foreign Policy Committee, "that our first task must be to erect a barrier against
aggression in Eastern Europe on behalf of states directly menaced by Germany. Until that barrier had been erected it was
clear that we ought to do nothing to impair the confidence of
those states." With respect to the Russians, Halifax concluded
that "we ought to play for time." [80] Cadogan's description of this
meeting is concise: "Meeting of F.P.C. at 11 about reply to
Soviet. Didn't last long—all agreed to turn them down." [81]

The British did not reply to the Soviet proposal until May
8, three weeks after it was made. Those three weeks gave
Stalin ample evidence that the British had no real intention of
fighting for Eastern Europe. First, Halifax responded on April
29 to Moscow's inquiries of April 16 and 17 about British determination to fight. He instructed Seeds to convey the following
to Litvinov:

> I do not understand why . . . Soviet Government should
> affect to believe that His Majesty's Government are not com-
> mitted by declarations they have made to Poland and Ru-
> mania. The language of those declarations . . . makes it clear
> that in the event of any action being taken which clearly
> threatened the independence of these countries and which the
> latter considered it vital to resist, His Majesty's Government
> would feel themselves bound at once to lend them all support
> in their power. The first condition is that there should be re-
> sistance to a clear threat to national independence.[82]

80. Colvin, p. 205.
81. Dilks, pp. 176–77.
82. DBFP, 5: 368.

This response really says the opposite of what it pretends to say. It proves that the British did not interpret their guarantees to Poland and Rumania as automatically requiring aid in the event of German aggression.[83] The aggression must constitute "a clear threat to national independence." Certainly this provided Britain with a loophole should she decide, for example, that a German ultimatum on Danzig did not pose a "clear threat" to Polish independence. Furthermore, as the British had always admitted, their commitment held only in the event that the threatened nation decided to resist German aggression. With such a condition stipulated by the nation that had forced Czechoslovakia to accede to German demands and had *obstructed* Czech resistance—the same nation that spoke in terms of using "threats" against Poland to insure her adherence to the former's wishes, any such guarantee was dubious indeed.

Seeds spoke with Litvinov on the morning of May 3, the last day the latter served as Foreign Minister before being replaced by Molotov. Litvinov asked the British Ambassador "whether there would be a declaration of war by His Majesty's Government in the event of aggression." Seeds's reply could only have added to Soviet doubts: "I said that declarations of war were rather out of fashion these days but that under promises made to Poland and other countries an aggressor on such a country which resisted a clear threat to national independence would find himself in at any rate a state of war with Great Britain." [84] To begin with, Seeds avoided Litvinov's question. Litvinov did not ask if there would be a declaration of war in the event that a guaranteed country resisted a clear threat; he asked only about the case of aggression, and said nothing about whether or not the country chose to resist. Even so, Britain's apparent unwillingness to commit herself to a declaration of war in fulfillment of her guarantee must have further impressed the Soviets as to

83. Halifax described even more reservations in the British guarantee in a letter of May 2, 1939, to the British Ambassador in Warsaw. See DBFP, 5: 401–2.
84. Ibid., p. 400.

the reluctance of England and France to fight in Eastern Europe.

On May 4, Churchill spoke in the House of Commons and strongly urged his Government to accept the Soviet terms, and to spare no time in doing so:

> The British people . . . have a right, in conjunction with the French Republic, to call upon Poland not to place obstacles in the way of a common cause. Not only must the full cooperation of Russia be accepted, but the three Baltic States, Lithuania, Latvia, and Estonia, must also be brought into association. . . . There is no means of maintaining an Eastern European Front against Nazi aggression without the active aid of Russia. Russian interests are deeply concerned in preventing Herr Hitler's designs on Eastern Europe. It should still be possible to range all the states and peoples from the Baltic to the Black Sea in one solid front against a new outrage or invasion. Such a front, if established in good heart, and with resolute and efficient military arrangements, combined with the strength of the Western Powers, may yet confront Hitler . . . and Company with forces the German people would be reluctant to challenge.[85]

The British Government finally replied to the Soviet proposal on May 8. The terms of the original British proposal for a unilateral Soviet declaration were simply repeated, with the addition of one new clause that would make Soviet acceptance even more unlikely. Now the British proposed that

> the Soviet Government should make a public declaration . . . in which, after referring to the . . . statements recently made by His Majesty's Government and the French Government accepting new obligations on behalf of certain Eastern European countries, the Soviet Government would undertake that in the event of Great Britain and France being involved in hostilities in fulfillment of these obligations, the assistance of the Soviet Government would be available, if desired, and would be afforded in such a manner and on such terms as might be agreed.[86]

85. Churchill, p. 365.
86. DBFP, 5: 357–59.

As Seeds emphasized to Molotov when he presented this proposal, "Soviet assistance would only be called for in the event of Great Britain and France being involved in hostilities in fulfillment of their obligations." [87] The Russians had already rejected a proposal by which they were committed to render unilateral aid only in the event that Poland or Rumania decided to resist German aggression and requested Russian aid. Now the British were asking the Russians to accept the same terms with the further limitation that Britain *and* France would have to be involved in war before Russian aid could be offered. In questioning Seeds about the proposal, Molotov focused on the ambiguous provision that aid be rendered "on such terms as might be agreed." According to Seeds's record of the meeting:

> To his question whether it was not intended that military conversations should begin at once, I answered that I thought on the whole such talks were envisioned only as a later development if events called for it; our main idea was that the issue by the Soviet Government of the proposed Declaration would so steady the European situation as not to require any other immediate steps for the moment.[88]

Seeds could hardly have been more explicit in telling the Russians that the British proposal was not intended as a realistic preparation for defense against aggression, but was instead a way to give the British a diplomatic edge in dealing with Hitler.

On May 11, Maisky met with Halifax and voiced some of the Soviet's objections to the British proposal. He concentrated on the need for definite military plans and probed Halifax on Anglo-French military preparations, suggesting that Anglo-French intervention under the recent guarantees could be delayed by last-minute conversations between each country's General Staffs. Halifax recorded that "to this I replied that our guarantee to Poland and Rumania involved us in coming immediately to their assistance, if our conditions were fulfilled,

87. Ibid., pp. 483–87.
88. Ibid.

and that, if words meant anything, it was impossible for us to give any assurance more complete." [89] Halifax was being evasive. The experience of the previous year had demonstrated that guarantees and alliances were without meaning unless backed by definite military commitments and prearranged plans for action. So, if the British and the French had made the military plans necessary to live up to their guarantee, it would have been quite possible for Halifax to give the Soviets an assurance "more complete." Yet, Halifax could not even assure his own countrymen on this same issue. In the House of Commons on May 19 Churchill complained:

> I want to draw the attention of the Committee to the fact that the question posed by Mr. Lloyd George ten days ago and repeated today has not been answered. The question was whether the General Staff was consulted before this guarantee [to Poland] was given as to whether it was safe and practical to give it, and whether there were any means of implementing it. The whole country knows that the question had been asked, and it has not been answered. That is disconcerting and disquieting.[90]

The Russians replied to the British proposal on May 14. They explained that "the English proposals do not contain the principle of reciprocity with regard to the U.S.S.R. and place the latter in a position of inequality as they do not contemplate an obligation by England and France to guarantee the U.S.S.R. in the event of a direct attack on the latter by aggressors." Furthermore, the Russians stated, because the English proposal covered only Poland and Rumania, the "north western frontier of the U.S.S.R. towards Finland, Estonia and Latvia remains uncovered," which could "serve to provoke aggression in the direction of the Soviet Union" in that area. In order to provide an effective barrier against further aggression in Europe, the Russians once more insisted that three conditions would have to be met:

89. Ibid., pp. 528–29.
90. Churchill, p. 375.

(1) The conclusion between England and France and U.S.S.R. of an effective pact of mutual assistance against aggression; (2) The guaranteeing by these three Great Powers of States of Central and Eastern Europe threatened by aggression including also Latvia, Estonia, and Finland. (3) The conclusion of a concrete agreement between England, France and U.S.S.R. as to forms and extent of assistance to be rendered materially to each other and to the guaranteed States.[91]

As one historian has noted, these three conditions "corresponded to the first three articles of the treaty proposed by Litvinov on April 17." [92] The Russians had not changed their terms.

On May 22, Maisky met with Halifax at Geneva, where both were attending a League meeting. Maisky said that the weakness of the British plan was that "it was based on a guarantee to Poland and Rumania alone." If either country or any of the Baltic states allowed the passage of German troops or the establishment of German air fields for an attack on Russia, Britain would not be obligated to act. Maisky stressed that the "essential thing was to prevent war." Here he seemed to repeat what Churchill had said earlier in the House of Commons: "[the] Soviet Government thought this could be done but only by organizing such a combination of forces that Germany would not dare to attack. . . . A triple pact was necessary and [the British] proposal entirely ignored this element in Soviet proposal." [93] On the same day, Maisky had a similar conversation with Bonnet and declared that his government would accept no agreement unless it featured a promise of direct British assistance.[94]

Pressure for an alliance with Russia was mounting on the British Government. France was determined to reach an accord, although not quite on Soviet terms. Prior to the British response of May 8, Bonnet had revealed to the Russian Ambassador in Paris France's desire for a triple alliance. Seeds was enraged at this "gross and deliberate error of tactics," and Soviet suspicions of British sincerity were aroused by this clear discrepancy be-

91. DBFP, 5: 558–59.
92. McSherry, p. 168.
93. DBFP, 5: 630–31.
94. McSherry, p. 169.

tween the French and British negotiating positions.[95] Halifax met with Bonnet and Daladier in Paris on May 20 to discuss the Anglo-French response to the Soviet rejection of the proposal of May 8. The only alternative that they felt might be acceptable to the Soviets was a triple alliance requiring mutual assistance in the event one of the signatories was directly attacked or became involved in hostilities as a result of helping another state. Halifax told Daladier that "it was unlikely that His Majesty's Government would be able to accept such a draft" for fear that the alliance "might well provoke Germany to violent action" and "divide public opinion in Britain." Daladier was taken aback, for he found the draft proposal "quite acceptable" and "could not understand Britain's difficulties." [96]

Pressure for an alliance with Russia was mounting in Parliament. The issue was debated in the House of Commons on May 19, and the exchange of views is quite illuminating. Lloyd George opened the discussion with an emotional appeal for alliance. He cited evidence that the Dictators were clearly involved in preparations for war, not for defense from aggression. He raised the familiar point that without Russia Britain could do nothing to save Poland or Rumania. "There has been a campaign of detraction of the Russian Army, Russian resources, Russian capacity, and Russian leadership," he alleged, pointing out the reluctance "to acknowledge the tremendous change which has occurred in Russia industrially and militarily." Citing statistics on Russian industrial output and air and tank power, George stated, "They are offering to place all this at the disposal of the Allies provided they are treated on equal terms. . . . Why is that not done?" [97]

In his reply, Chamberlain accused Lloyd George of fabricating an unnecessarily gloomy picture, and outlined his policy:

> The assurances which gave to Poland . . . Rumania, and to Greece were . . . what one might call first-aid treatment given to avoid any further deterioration of the situation. It still

95. Ibid., p. 292; Thorne, pp. 140–41.
96. DBFP, 5: 623–25.
97. Namier, pp. 165–67; Churchill, pp. 371–73.

remains to strengthen them by more permanent arrangements and to try to get more support for them from any other quarters that are able and willing to give that support. I want to make it clear that this policy is not a policy of lining up opposing blocs of Powers in Europe animated by hostile intentions toward one another, and accepting the view that war is inevitable. . . . We are always trying to avoid this policy of what I call opposing blocs, because it seems to us to be essentially an unstable policy . . . the direct participation of the Soviet Union in this matter might not be altogether in accordance with the wishes of some of the countries . . . we are trying to build up, not an alliance between ourselves and other countries, but a peace front against aggression, and we should not be succeeding in that policy if, by ensuring cooperation of one country, we rendered another country uneasy and unwilling to cooperate with us.[98]

Chamberlain was still hinding behind the stubbornness of the Polish junta and Rumanian monarchy; that he could rate the value of Soviet military power on the same level as that of Poland and Rumania revealed what Churchill charitably called a "lack of proportion." [99] Furthermore, Chamberlain was deceitful when he spoke of his opposition to a policy of creating "opposing blocs." This *was* his policy when he was courting Germany, but now he was using opposition to the principle to stall an agreement with Russia.

Churchill voiced his strong disagreement with the Prime Minister's statement of policy:

If you are ready to be an ally of Russia in time of war . . . if you are ready to join hands with Russia in the defense of Poland, which you have guaranteed, and of Rumania, why should you shrink from becoming the ally of Russia now, when you may by that very fact prevent the breaking-out of war? I cannot understand all these refinements of diplomacy and delay. If the worst comes to the worst, you are in the midst of it with them, and you have to make the best of it with them. If the difficulties do not arise, well, you will have had the security in the preliminary stages. . . .

98. Namier, pp. 167–68.
99. Churchill, p. 373.

Clearly Russia is not going to enter into agreements unless she is treated as an equal, and . . . has confidence that the methods employed by the Allies—by the peace front—are such as would be likely to lead to success. . . . Unless there is an eastern front set up, what is going to happen to the West? . . . Without an effective eastern front, there can be no satisfactory defense of our interests in the West, and without Russia there can be no effective eastern front.[100]

Churchill was candid: Great Britain needed Russia's help to absorb enough of the German military might that Britain and France would be able to defend themselves in the West. Chamberlain and Halifax were sensitive to the need for an eastern front, but they were banking first on the belief that their current policy was sufficient to deter Hitler and then, in the event that Hitler struck, that Poland and Rumania could provide at least enough resistance to tie up Hitler militarily in the east. They were still unwilling to pay the price for an alliance with Russia.

Pressure for a triple alliance including Russia was also coming from the military and the Foreign Office. At a meeting of the Foreign Policy Committee on May 5, there was presented an aide-memoire by the Chiefs of Staff in which a significantly new position was expressed. The Chiefs, as was not uncommon, argued on political as well as military grounds. Now, as they reasoned, the advantages, both diplomatic and military, of a mutual alliance with Russia outweighed the disadvantages: "we should gain more than we should lose" by giving Russia a guarantee of assistance in the event of a direct attack or an attack through the Baltic states. Chamberlain argued against the Chiefs, implying that they had not appreciated that an arrangement such as they advocated would not be possible without a full alliance. The central fear of the Chiefs, which emerged in the debate, was that Russia would become allied with Germany. Halifax also opposed the Chiefs, and suggested that they were unduly influenced by Russia's pushy attitude; he "felt the

100. Ibid., pp. 374–76. See also Eden's speech advocating alliance in Eden, *The Reckoning*, pp. 64, 647–49.

greatest reluctance to being bluffed off a good and sound policy by Russian insistence." [101] By May 16 Cadogan, Strang, and Harvey were coming around to the position that Britain would have to agree to a triple pact. On May 20, Cadogan dictated a Foreign Office paper for the Cabinet favoring an alliance, but presenting the case "warily" because he knew Chamberlain "hated" the idea: "In his present mood, P.M. says he will resign rather than sign alliance with Soviet." [102] On May 20, Halifax told Harvey that Chamberlain "was very reluctant to agree to full tripartite alliance, although many in the Cabinet favoured it." The same day Strang speculated to Harvey "that what is in the back of P.M.'s mind, and especially of Horace Wilson's, is that appeasement will be dead after this. He says that all at No. 10 [Downing St.] are anti-Soviet." [103]

Events of May 22 forced a change in the British position. On that day the German and Italian Foreign Ministers signed the "Pact of Steel," a military alliance in which the two countries promised mutual aid should either become involved in war. The same day, Cadogan submitted his memorandum, arguing, as Churchill did a few days before, that if an eastern front "built up on Poland" were to collapse in the event of war, Hitler would be free to strike in the West. "Therefore," the memorandum continued, "it might be claimed that a tripartite pact with the Soviet Union, if that is the only means by which we can be assured of the latter's support, is a necessary condition for the consolidation of the front which we have been trying to create." The memorandum admitted that in spite of all the profound doubts about Russia's willingness or capability to fulfill her commitments under such a treaty, "the alternative of a Soviet Union completely untrammelled and exposed continually to the temptation of intriguing with both sides" was a greater danger.[104] It was also on this day that Halifax spoke with Maisky

101. Colvin, pp. 212–13.
102. Dilks, pp. 180–82.
103. Harvey, p. 290.
104. DBFP, 5: 645–47.

at Geneva. After that conversation the Foreign Secretary wrote that the choice was "disagreeably plain": either there would be a complete and formal alliance or the negotiations would break down.[105] Now the British could not forfeit the opportunity for a commitment of Soviet aid.

This is not to say, however, that the British had decided to agree to Soviet terms. Rather, they tried to work out a proposal that might satisfy Soviet concerns as expressed in their April 17 proposal and still deny the Russians a free hand in the Balkans or Eastern Europe. As Halifax explained to Kennedy on May 24, Russian terms would have to be accepted, "but, in order that the humiliation will not be too great in having to step down from their original plan and accept the Russian's plan, they have decided to put it under the cloak of the League platform of anti-aggression and bring in Poland and Turkey and all the rest under the same canopy." [106] The Cabinet meeting of May 24, which produced a decision to offer the Russians an alliance under the Covenant of the League, also confirmed the suspicion that Strang had expressed to Harvey four days earlier, that Chamberlain feared an alliance with Russia would preclude any further appeasement. Thomas Inskip, in his capacity as Secretary of State for the Dominions, made the suggestion that "when we had strengthened our position by making an agreement with the Russian Government we should take the iniative in a renewal of the search for appeasement. . . . We should be in a position to make such an approach from strength. . . . There was more likelihood that Germany would be willing to listen. . . . We might indicate that we . . . were ready at any time to discuss any matters in dispute." Inskip indicated that this suggestion "had a good deal in common" with a recent statement by Halifax to the German Ambassador Dirksen; Halifax confirmed that at their most recent meeting he had told Dirksen that, in spite of Britain's warnings and increased armaments, "there was, however, also a positive side to our policy." Chamberlain felt

105. Ibid., p. 634.
106. FRUS (1939), 1: 259–60.

Inskip's idea "premature," but clearly stated that "he did not reject the suggestion." [107]

The new Anglo-French proposal, for which the British were responsible, was delivered to the Russians on May 27. The proposal was framed within the Covenant of the League and was a clever attempt to avoid almost every commitment deemed vital by the Soviets, while appearing to do the opposite. Its relevant provisions were as follows:

> The Governments of the United Kingdom, France and the U.S.S.R. desiring to give effect, *in their capacity of Member of the League of Nations,* to the principle of mutual support against aggression which is embodied in the Covenant of the League, have reached the following agreement:
> I. If France and the United Kingdom *are engaged in hostilities* with a European Power, in consequence of either (1) aggression by that Power against another European State which they had, *in conformity with the wishes of that State,* undertaken to assist against such aggression, (2) assistance given by them to another European State *which had requested such assistance* in order to resist a violation of its neutrality, or (3) aggression by a European Power against either France or the United Kingdom, the U.S.S.R., *acting in accordance with the principles of Article 16, paragraphs 1 and 2, of the Covenant of the League of Nations,* will give France and the United Kingdom all the support and assistance in its power. (emphasis added)

Article II was identical except that it provided for Anglo-French aid to Russia should the latter become engaged in hostilities.

> III. The three governments will concert together as to the methods by which such mutual support and assistance could, in the case of need, be made most effective.
> IV. In the event of circumstances arising which threaten to call their undertakings of mutual support and assistance into operation, the three Governments will immediately consult together upon the situation. The methods and scope of such consultation will at once be the subject of further discussion between the three Governments.

107. Colvin, pp. 225–26.

V. It is understood that the rendering of support and assistance in the above cases is without prejudice to the rights and position of other Powers.[108]

Within the context of the spring and summer of 1939, this proposal amounted to something short of a commitment for mutual aid between the three Powers. According to Article II, Britain and France were obligated to aid Russia only if she were (1) directly attacked, or (2) went to war over aggression against another State either because of an obligation "in conformity with the wishes of that State," or because the State "had requested such assistance." There was not a single country along Russia's borders that would have desired a military alliance with the Soviet Union; as I have previously discussed, the case was exactly the opposite. Hence Britain and France were offering to aid Russia under conditions that apparently had no chance of materializing, whereas Russia would be obligated to aid Britain and France automatically by virtue of their mutual guarantees to Poland, Rumania, and Greece, as well as in Western Europe. To make matters worse, should the circumstance arise by which Britain and France could be held to their obligation to aid Russia, they were bound to do so only "in accordance with the principles of Article 16, paragraphs 1 and 2" of the League Covenant. Molotov was not without justification when he immediately protested that such dependence upon the League would render the agreement ineffective: "He put it that the British and French were prepared to visualize Moscow being bombed by an aggressor while Bolivia was busy blocking all action in Geneva." Seeds tried to dispel Molotov's fears by arguing that the emphasis of the British proposal was meant to be on the principles rather than the procedures of the League.[109] Yet there was nothing in the draft itself to guarantee that this ambiguous distinction would be made when it really mattered, that is, when the time came for decision to go to war. If any-

108. DBFP, 5:688–89.
109. Ibid., pp. 710–12.

thing, the draft implied that, since the three Powers were acting "in their capacity of Member of the League," they would be bound to act through the League in fulfilling their obligations under this agreement. Likewise, by singling out paragraphs 1 and 2 of Article 16, which contain general references to condemnatory steps and a provision that the League Council "recommend" military action to be taken in the event of aggression,[110] the draft proposal prevented invoking paragraph 3 of Articles 16 and 17, which deal with provisions for fellow members granting the right of passage for troops to aid another member.[111]

Molotov also protested that the proposal "evaded the third of the three essential points, the conclusion of a concrete agreement as to the forms and extent of assistance to be rendered mutually. [112] Two days later, Molotov reminded Seeds that "the French-Soviet Pact had turned out to be merely a paper delusion; experience in that respect had taught the Soviet Government the absolute necessity in practice to conclude, simultaneously, both a political and military agreement." [113] Molotov was right. The Anglo-French proposal not only insisted that the political agreement must precede any military arrangements, but Article IV of the new draft specifically postponed military consultations until "the event of circumstances arising which threaten to call their undertakings of mutual support and assistance into operation." A state along Russia's border could be threatened, invaded, and overcome before the British, French, and Soviet General Staffs even met to begin talking about what military action to take.

Finland, Latvia, Estonia, and Lithuania all refused to be included in a general guarantee of which Russia was a part. On March 31, Finland and Estonia further stipulated that such a guarantee extended to them would be interpreted as an act of aggression. On the same day Estonia and Latvia signed non-

110. Carr, p. 288.
111. Thorne, p. 142.
112. DBFP, 5: 710–12.
113. Ibid., pp. 725–27.

aggression pacts with Germany.[114] For Soviet Russia, the situation became more threatening. A formal response to the Anglo-French proposal of May 27 had to be formulated. In their response of June 2, the Soviets offered a "modification" of the May 27 draft; this modification was in fact a repetition of the terms Moscow had first asked on April 17, amended to correct the deficiencies of the Anglo-French draft and offering a major concession.

The preamble of the June 2 Soviet proposal corrected the Anglo-French invocation of the League Covenant by stipulating that the three Powers had concluded the agreement "with the object of making more effective the principles of mutual assistance against aggression adopted by the League of Nations." With this, both the British and the Soviets could have their "cake." Article I of the June 2 draft required mutual aid in the event a signatory became involved in war as a result of (1) "aggression by [a European] Power against any one of these three States"; (2) "aggression by that Power against Belgium, Greece, Turkey, Rumania, Poland, Latvia, Estonia and Finland, whom England, France and U.S.S.R. have agreed to defend against aggression"; or (3) assistance to another European State that had requested such assistance in order to resist aggression. According to Article II, "The three States will come to an agreement within the shortest possible time as to methods, forms and extent of assistance which is to be rendered by them in conformity with paragraph I." Also of concern here is Article VI: "The present agreement enters into force simultaneously with agreement which is to be concluded in virtue of paragraph II." [115]

The major difference between this Soviet proposal and the original one of April 17 is that now the Russians offered to commit themselves to aid Britain and France in areas not vital to Soviet security. Except for Belgium and Greece, the countries included in the list in Article I were obviously included in the April

114. Churchill, pp. 379–80.
115. DBFP, 5: 753–54.

17 proposal by the designation "Eastern European States situated between Baltic and Black Seas and bordering on the U.S.S.R." The specific mention of Belgium, Greece, Turkey, Poland, and Rumania made it clear that the Soviets were proposing a genuinely mutual agreement, because the British and French had already identified their own national interests with the defense of these nations. Furthermore, section (3) of Article I provided for mutual aid to other European States that requested it, which would include States unnamed in the agreement that were vital to Britain's and France's defense. This represented a significant Soviet concession by agreeing to take on mutual obligations in Western Europe; the original Soviet proposal involved only Eastern Europe. The Soviets made this concession no doubt to lend weight to their arguments in favor of committing the British and the French to an area vital to Soviet interests—the Baltic. As Churchill wrote in the *New York Herald-Tribune* on June 7, 1939:

> The Russian claim that Finland and the Baltic States should be included in the triple guarantee is well founded. . . . People say, "What if they do not wish to be guaranteed?" It is certain, however, that if Lithuania, Latvia, and Estonia were invaded by the Nazis or subverted to the Nazi system by propaganda and intrigue from within, the whole of Europe would be dragged into war.[116]

On June 7, Chamberlain told the House of Commons that he was sending a representative of the Foreign Office to Moscow with the hope of speeding the negotiations. This was done in place of calling home Seeds, who was bedridden with influenza, for consultations. The man sent to Moscow was William Strang, head of the Central Department of the Foreign Office. As one historian has commented, "the sending of a comparatively junior official of the Foreign Office, however able and experienced, on a mission of such paramount importance was surprising." [117] Churchill's judgment was more severe: "the sending

116. Namier, p. 181.
117. Ibid., p. 184.

of so subordinate a figure gave actual offense." [118]

In his speech to the Commons on June 7, Chamberlain mentioned a problem implicit in preparing to resist "aggression". The British, he said,

> have made it clear that they are ready, immediately and without any reserve, to join with the French Government in giving the U.S.S.R. full military support in the event of any act of aggression against her in hostilities with a European Power. It is not intended that the military support which the three Powers would agree to extend to one another should be confined to a case of actual aggression upon their territory. It is possible to imagine various cases in which one of the three Governments might feel that its security was indirectly menaced by the action of another European Power.[119]

On the following day, June 8, Halifax requested a meeting with Maisky in which he specifically drew attention to Chamberlain's June 7 statement and made it "plain" that the guarantee to Russia contemplated by the British Government "was not confined only to a direct attack upon Soviet territory,"[120] Maisky informed Halifax on June 12 that "it was an indispensable condition for any agreement that steps should be taken to meet the indirect menace to Soviet security. The crux of the matter lay . . . in securing agreement on the substance of the problem raised by direct or indirect aggression against the Baltic States." [121]

Strang arrived in Moscow on June 14, bringing with him a new British draft, a detailed memorandum on the British position, and written instructions for Seeds. The following day, he, Seeds, and Naggier, the French Ambassador, met with Molotov to resume the negotiations and present new British proposals. The major British objection to the Soviet proposal of June 2 was the naming of the states to be guaranteed; the British proposed that instead, the agreement should provide that in the case of

118. Churchill, p. 389.
119. DBFP. 5: 787–88.
120. Ibid., 6: 6.
121. Ibid., 50–51.

states not already guaranteed, namely, the Baltic states, "the three Powers should consult together if one of them considered that its security was menaced by a threat to the independnce or neutrality of any other European Power. If the other two Powers agreed that such a menace existed, and if the contracting Power in question was involved in hostilities in consequence, the other two Powers would go to its assistance." [122]

On June 16, Molotov presented the formal Soviet reply, stating that the Soviets could not tie their hands as the Anglo-French proposal suggested. Russia was being asked to come to the aid of Poland, Rumania, Belgium, Greece, and Turkey if any of these countries were attacked, but Britain and France were unwilling to undertake similar obligations to Russia in the event of aggression against Finland, Estonia, and Latvia. The Russians suggested, in "view of the existence of differences of opinion further discussion is necessary on the question of simultaneous entry into force of general agreement and military agreement." [123]

It is necessary at this point to outline the nature of Soviet-German contacts during this period of the negotiations. On June 2, in response to orders from Berlin, Hilger, Counsellor to the German Embassy in Moscow, contacted Mikoyan, the Soviet Foreign Trade Commissar, and assured the latter that Germany really desired economic agreement. Mikoyan pointed to the German obstruction of the negotiations in February and said that he was not interested in negotiating now, but would reply later. On June 8, Mikoyan told Hilger that the Soviet Government would receive Schnurre in Moscow if Berlin would accept the substance of the last Soviet economic proposal of February; he also stated that his government would consider a visit by Schnurre as a demonstration of Berlin's sincerity in the matter of "politics." Schulenburg, the German Ambassador to Moscow, met with Astakhov, the Soviet chargé in Berlin, on June 17 and conveyed Weizsacker's assurance that Germany did not intend to

122. Ibid., pp. 116–19.
123. Ibid., pp. 89–91.

attack Russia, but rather to normalize German-Soviet relations. Astakhov was concommittal, spoke of difficulties to be overcome, but expressed his opinion that good relations "could not but be advantageous to both countries." On the same day, in Moscow, Mikoyan received Hilger, who reported that Schnurre could visit Russia with the power to negotiate an economic agreement, but that Germany was unprepared to accept the Soviet proposal of February. Mikoyan replied that his conditions were not met. He recalled Hilger on June 25 to deliver a formal reply, which consisted of a request for the specific points on which German and Soviet views differed. While awaiting a response from Berlin, Schulenburg returned to Moscow and met with Molotov (at the former's request) on June 28. He was now prepared to give further assurances that Germany did not intend to attack Russia. Molotov repeated the previous Soviet request for more specific information from the Germans.[124]

At the same time, the intelligence received by the British and the French indicated that the only thing that could stop Hitler from attacking Poland was a triple alliance that included Russia. On June 1, Coulondre, now the French Ambassador to Berlin, reported that he had learned "if Poland does not yield, Herr Hitler's decision will depend upon the signature of the Anglo-Russian pact. It is believed that he will risk war if he does not have to fight Russia, but that if, on the contrary, he knows that he will have to fight Russia as well, he will give way." [125] On June 8, Daladier told British Ambassador Phipps about Coulondre's report, and Phipps wired London that Daladier felt "further delay may even be dangerous and encourage Herr Hitler to seize Danzig before we reach an agreement with the Soviet. . . . M. Daladier therefore feels that we must rope in Russia as soon as possible." [126] On June 13, Coulondre reported that Ribbentrop was convinced that the only feasible thing to do with Poland was to divide it between Germany and Russia:

124. This account is based on McSherry, pp. 154–59.
125. Ibid., p. 182.
126. DBFP, 6: 2.

"He will not abandon [this idea] until the Anglo-Russian pact
is signed." [127] On June 15, Erich Kordt, Ribbentrop's private
secretary, while on vacation in London sent word to the British
Foreign Office through an intermediary that Moscow and Berlin
were in contact. He offered his view "that an Anglo-Russian
agreement would be a strong deterrent to war, and that a failure
of the negotiations with Moscow would be a great temptation to
the Central Powers to risk another move." [128] At the end of June,
the Kordt brothers spoke with Sir Robert Vansittart, a chief
British diplomatic adviser, and informed him that, to their personal knowledge, Hitler was ready to make a deal with Russia
to free him for war against Poland and then the West, whereas
if an Anglo-Soviet agreement were concluded, he would "sum-
mon a party congress of peace in the fall." [129]

Thus, at the same time that the British and French were
feeling the pressure to conclude an agreement with Russia,
Russia was receiving signals that Hitler was willing to make a
deal with her. As a result, both sides now negotiated in a new
context. For Britain and France, the problem was to find a formula acceptable to the Soviets that would not serve as a blue-
print for or acknowledgment of Soviet predominance in Eastern
Europe. As Bonnet told William Bullitt on June 5, "France and
England could certainly not consent to giving the Soviet Union
support for an extension of Bolshevism in Eastern Europe." [130]
For her part, Moscow remained extremely cautious and tentative
about negotiating with the Germans until the latter part of July.
Schulenburg analyzed Soviet motives on June 25:

> Mikoyan does not want to see the talks with us broken
> off, but wishes to keep the negotiations firmly in hand, in
> order to determine their course at any time. Obviously it
> would not at present fit into the framework of the Soviet
> Government's general policy if a sensation were to be created
> by a resumption of the economic negotiations.[131]

127. McSherry, p. 182.
128. DBFP, 6: 705.
129. McSherry, p. 183.
130. FRUS (1939) 1: 266–69.
131. DGFP, 6: 790–91.

As late as July 10, Schulenburg felt that Moscow wished to keep in contact with Berlin, but "at the moment, they are still chary of entering into actual economic negotiations which could not be concealed from the public." [132] Moscow still seemed to attach more importance to its negotiations with Britain and France, and the knowledge that Hitler was looking to make a deal doubtlessly elevated Stalin's confidence that he could get exactly what he was asking from the British and French Governments. There is no evidence that Stalin was ever willing to accept anything *less* than his original terms, and, faced with the combined forces of Anglo-French efforts to alter and mollify the Soviet proposal and German feelers for a non-aggression pact, he insisted that Britain and France accept a more explicit, better-defined version of the April 17 proposal; he never deviated from the substance of that proposal except to extend his commitments past Eastern Europe as a gesture to the West.

On June 19, Halifax instructed Seeds to assure Molotov that Britain was willing to take part in a guarantee of the Baltic States if this could be done without naming them or appearing to force a highly distasteful guarantee upon them.[133] When Seeds and Naggier met with Moltov again on June 21, they presented a new British draft of Article I: The other two countries would at once furnish all possible support should one of the three become involved in hostilities with a European Power as a result of: "(1) aggression by that Power against any one of these three countries, or aggression by it which, being directed against another European State, thereby constituted a menace to the security of one of these three countries, or (2) aggression by that Power against another European State which the contracting country concerned had, with the approval of that State, undertaken to assist against such aggression." [134] As Halifax admitted to Seeds, this new proposal differed only in language from the British draft prsented on June 15, "since no party can impose on the others its own view of what constitutes a menace, and

132 Ibid., pp. 928–29.
133. DBFP, 6: 103–5.
134. Ibid., pp. 91–92, 140–42.

the question would really have to be settled by consultation." [135]
This was not lost on the Russians; Potemkin, Molotov's assistant,
immediately asked how it would be decided, according to the
new proposal, whether aggression against a European State constituted a menace to the security of one of the signatories. Molotov expressed the position of his government that there was no
alternative to naming the countries to be guaranteed, since it
would be virtually impossible to be prepared for the contingency
of having to aid every European State. Naggier suggested listing
the States to be guaranteed in a separate unpublished protocol,
and each party agreed to investigate that possibility. When
pressed for a Soviet counter-draft, Molotov at this meeting and
again the next day stated that the Soviet position was embodied
in their proposal of June 2.[136]

On June 24, Seeds wired Halifax that Moscow desired a
treaty in which mutual obligations were "set down in black and
white and to be clear beyond dispute." He also indicated that
Britain would have to deal with Moscow's fear, which he was
not willing to concede was genuine, "that the Baltic States
may voluntarily, or under pressure, move into the German orbit."
What the Russians wanted, Seeds wrote, was "to secure our
assistance or at the least apparent connivance should they ever
find it expedient to intervene in the Baltic States." [137] For the
Russians, a treaty with Britain and France could serve little
purpose unless it contained such a provision. Cadogan had addressed this point long before, in his May 22 memorandum: "If
the Soviet Government really entertain this fear [that Britain
would remain uncommitted in the event of a German attack on
Russia through the Baltic states], it is evident that we shall have
to undertake some commitment to allay it." [138] As Fontaine has
explained, "From the point of view of Russian security, it would
seem indispensable to guard against the consequences of a bor-

135. Ibid., pp. 91–92.
136. Ibid., pp. 141–43.
137. Ibid., p. 161.
138. Ibid., 5: 639–47.

der country's rallying to the Axis. . . . What good did it do to protect the Polish and Rumanian borders if there was still a breach to the north through which the Nazis could sweep from one day to the next?" [139]

Seeds understood why Article I of the British proposal presented on June 21 was unacceptable to the Russians. As he explained to Halifax:

> Paragraph I of that [article] did not make it clear beyond question that the Baltic States would be fully covered. It did not specify who was to judge whether an act of aggression against the Baltic States constituted a menace to the security of the Soviet Union. This was a loophole through which Great Britain and France might evade their obligations to assist the Soviet Union. No such loophole for the Soviet Government seemed to exist in the second paragraph of our draft, since the mere fact of Great Britain and France becoming engaged in hostilities on behalf of a country to whom they had given a guarantee would apparently of itself bring into play the obligations of the Soviet Union to come to their assistance and the Soviet Government would have little voice in the matter.[140]

Seeds was well aware of the Soviet position, including their precise terms of June 2. Furthermore, he knew, as Halifax had pointed out, that the British proposal presented on June 21 was really the same as that of June 15, which had already been rejected by the Russians. As revealed in the above quotation, Seeds understood and appreciated the reasons why such a proposal was unacceptable to the Russians. Indeed, Molotov was not without justification "in his anxiety to make us understand that, in his view, the British and French Governments were treating the Russians as simpletons . . . and fools." [141]

On June 27, Halifax wired Seeds that he still wished "to avoid any mention of States," but that if "a nominal roll of States" were necessary to secure Soviet agreement, he "should

139. Fontaine, pp. 109–10.
140. DBFP, 6: 162.
141. Ibid., p. 119.

infinitely prefer" a secret, unpublished list. Accordingly, Halifax submitted a new draft of Article I, which contained a curious ploy. The new draft read as follows:

> The United Kingdom, France and the U.S.S.R. undertake to give to each other immediately all effective assistance should one of these countries become involved in hostilities with a European Power as a result of aggression by that Power against any one of these three countries, or aggression by it against another European State which the contracting country concerned felt obliged to assist in maintaining its independence or neutrality against such aggression.[142]

As Halifax's wire to Seeds indicates, the latter part of the revised article I, providing only for aid to States that a contracting country "felt obliged to assist," was intended to replace sections "(2) and (3) in Article I of M. Molotov's draft of June 2." In connection with this, Halifax insisted that the list of States to be guaranteed include Switzerland and the Netherlands. Yet, section (3) in Article I of Molotov's June 2 draft provided for mutual aid to any European State outside of the eight States listed that desired help in the event of aggression against it. This provision clearly covered British and French interests in Western Europe, because both countries had cordial relationships with and commitments to the countries on Germany's Western border. However, this provision alone was not sufficient to cover Soviet needs because Russia's relationship with her bordering States was not friendly—hence the need for a specific list. When shown Halifax's new draft of Article I, Naggier immediately took exception to it because, (1) the Russians could be expected to resist the specific inclusion of Holland and Switzerland, countries with which they did not have diplomatic relations, and (2) the omission of section (3) of Article I of the Soviet's June 2 draft and its replacement with a list of selected countries seriously limited Anglo-French freedom of action and deprived the proposed agreement of the "necessary elasticity" that might be of

142. Ibid., pp. 173–74.

use in an unforeseen contingency. Seeds wrote that "there is certainly some force in this argument." [143] Halifax stuck to his previous position, arguing that, for unspecified reasons, the Soviet draft of Article I (3) was not "a satisfactory method of dealing with Holland and Switzerland." [144]

The historian can only speculate on Halifax's motives for dropping Article I(3). The evidence that this was motivated by legitimate Anglo-French interests is unpersuasive, and, to jump ahead a bit, Halifax was soon willing to accept the omission of *both* I (3) *and* mention of Holland and Switzerland. In context, Halifax's ploy appears to have been a delaying tactic. In a Cabinet meeting on June 20, Chamberlain expressed his confidence that he could secure an agreement with Russia whenever he wanted and that the best policy would be to drive a hard bargain so that the Russians would not think the British were over-anxious for an agreement. On June 27, the day he sent his new draft to Seeds, Halifax told Joseph Kennedy that he and his Government were inclined "to tell Russia to go jump into the Baltic Sea or any other sea they can find, except that they have been under constant pressure from all their friends who say that the failure of a Russian pact would be psychologically bad for England." [145] Perhaps Zhdanov was on the right track when he wrote in Pravda two days later, "It seems to me that the English and French do not want a real agreement or one acceptable to the U.S.S.R.: the only thing they really want is to talk about an agreement and, by making play with the obstinacy of the Soviet Union, to prepare their own public opinion for an eventual deal with the aggressors." [146]

When Seeds and Naggier presented the new proposal to Molotov on July 1, the predictable happened. Molotov said that the draft "was too vague and that it would be necessary to give it precision by adding" a list of States. Seeds suggested that the

143. Ibid., pp. 208–9.
144. Ibid., p. 225.
145. Aster, p. 269; FRUS (1939), 1: 276.
146. DBFP, 6: 219.

list "be embodied in an unpublished annex to the Treaty" and Molotov indicated that his Government would agree to this. Seeds then submitted a draft of the secret protocol, containing the following list: "Estonia and Finland and Latvia, Poland and Rumania and Turkey and Greece and Belgium and Luxemburg and the Netherlands and Switzerland." Molotov immediately remarked that "it would be difficult if not impossible for the Soviet Government to accept obligations in respect of Netherlands and Switzerland" because it "had no diplomatic relations with these two countries." Seeds noted that Molotov "did not seem to bother much about Luxemburg." [147]

In the course of the conversation, Molotov raised another objection to the new draft of Article I: "It did not make provision for cases of indirect aggression." He suggested a revision so that Article I would explicitly provide for action in the event of direct or indirect aggression by one European Power against another which any of the signatories felt obliged to resist. Seeds and Naggier told Molotov that "this was a new point." This was not exactly true; Chamberlain, as early as June 7, had announced his government's willingness and intention to sign an agreement covering indirect aggression, and Maisky had warned Halifax on June 12 that provision for indirect aggression "was an indispensable conditions for any agreement." (Halifax had wired this information to Seeds.) Nevertheless, British records indicate that the issue of indirect aggression had not been brought up in the negotiations in Moscow, and in that sense it could be called "a new point," or perhaps, more precisely, a point that as of then had not been, but would inevitably have to be, discussed.

It is fairly obvious why Molotov raised the issue of indirect aggression at this point. The British and French had reached the point where they were willing to agree to most of the basic Soviet terms; as Seeds told Molotov at the July 1 session, "our new draft gave the Soviet Government everything they had asked for in their own draft." Seeds was careless in this state-

147. Ibid., pp. 229–32.

ment, however, for the British and French now held back on one important aspect of Article I—that the list of guaranteed countries be included in the published protocol. Now, to give the public version of the prospective treaty more force in the absence of specific mention of European States, the provision to act in the event of indirect aggression should be added. Indeed, Molotov told Seeds and Naggier on July 8 'that the absence of any reference to indirect aggression in Article I would deprive the Treaty of a good deal of its value as a deterrent to aggression." [148] At any rate, in view of the history of Hitlerian aggression, no agreement could go far enough toward protecting the security of Britain, France, and especially Russia unless it provided for a definite response to indirect aggression, and even Chamberlain had admitted this.

Molotov presented the formal reply of his government on July 4. The Soviets "agreed to inclusion of list of States in an unpublished protocol," but refused to include Luxemburg, the Netherlands, or Switzerland in the list. They further insisted that Article I mention indirect aggression, to be defined in the secret protocol as "an internal coup d'etat or a reversal of policy in the interests of the aggressor." [149]

On July 6, Halifax wired Seeds and outlined the limits of the concessions Britain was willing to make: "we agree to the omission of Holland, Switzerland and Luxemburg from the list of States," "we are prepared to have a list of the other States in the unpublished Protocol," and, "as regards indirect aggression we can go no further than" to allow a definition of the term in the secret protocol "only on condition that Article I should speak only of 'aggression' omitting words 'direct or indirect.'" Furthermore, the Soviet definition of indirect aggression "is completely unacceptable." Halifax suggested that Seeds propose that reference to indirect aggression be omitted from Article I and that the secret protocol contain the agreement "that the word 'aggression' (as used in Article I) is to be understood as covering action

148. Ibid., p. 309.
149. Ibid., p. 251.

accepted by the State in question under threat of force by another Power and involving the abandonment by it of its independence or neutrality." [150]

The formal Soviet reply to this new proposal was presented by Molotov on July 9: "The Soviet Government insist on the inclusion of the words 'direct or indirect' in Article I." Furthermore, the British definition of indirect aggression was rejected and a new Soviet definition offered:

> The expression "indirect aggression" covers action accepted by any of the [listed] States under threat of force by another Power, or without any such threat, involving the use of territory and forces of the State in question for purposes of aggression against that State or against one of the contracting parties, and consequently involving the loss of, by that State, its independence or violation of its neutrality.

This definition incorporated the British proposal that indirect aggression involved the "threat of force," and attempted to provide for the very possible contingency that a country could be used by another country, without the threat of force, to commit aggression against England, France, or Russia—for example, if Finland permitted the passage of German troops or establishment of German airfields for an attack on Russia. As an apparent gesture toward Britain and France, Russia now officially provided that Switzerland and the Netherlands could be included in the unpublished list in the event that the Western Powers reciprocated by making it possible for Russia to conclude "pacts of mutual assistance" with Poland and Turkey. Molotov reminded Seeds and Naggier that "it was absolutely essential in the view of the Soviet Government that these two Agreements [political and military] should not merely enter into force but also be signed simultaneously." This certainly was not a "new point," for the Russians had insisted on this point from the very beginning of the negotiations and had requested "further discussion" of it at the June 16 session in Moscow. However,

150. Ibid., pp. 276–77.

as late as July 9, Seeds and Naggier were unable to answer Molotov on this issue and both Ambassadors decided to negotiate no further without additional instructions from their governments.[151]

On July 15, Halifax wired new instructions to Seeds. He informed the Ambassador that the French Government had authorized Naggier to accept the words "direct or indirect" in Article I, and authorized him to "tell Molotov that we would be ready without further delay to start technical discussions," which would be "conditional upon M. Molotov abandoning his demand for simultaneous signature of the political and military Agreements."[152]

Molotov met with Seeds and Naggier on July 17, when he was informed by the latter two that a definition of indirect aggression could be published in Article I if it did not stipulate cases where a threat of force was not involved; the previous Soviet definition of indirect agrression was rejected. Molotov immediately termed the new definition unacceptable because it was too vague and restricted. Indeed, the British refusal to accept a definition of indirect aggression other than one involving a threat of force must have appeared as a delaying tactic to the Russians. The British guarantee to Poland spoke only of a threat to Poland's independence and made no qualification that the threat need involve mention of the use of force.Now the Moscow negotiations were virtually concluded on the matter of Article I, yet the British threatened to snag any further agreement by refusing to accept a condition for which they themselves had provided in their guarantee to Poland. At one point in the July 17 conversations, Seeds argued that Molotove should drop his request for simultaneous signing of the political and military agreements. Molotov remained firm; there would be only "a single Politico-Military Agreement. The political part would have no existence without the military agreement. The Soviet Government wished to have military obligations and contributions on each side clearly settled." Unless Britain and France

151. Ibid., pp. 310–13.
152. Ibid., p. 360.

could agree to this, "there was no point in pursuing the present conversations." Molotov then bluntly asked "whether or not His Majesty's Government and [the] French Government were really willing to open military conversations." Naggier felt that France would be ready to begin military negotiations without waiting for signature of the political agreement. Seeds equivocated that the political agreement should first be reached, but not necessarily signed. Molotov concluded by requesting that each Ambassador obtain a definite answer from his government.[153]

Why did Russia press for military talks now? The international situation was such that Moscow could no longer be content to wait until the British Foreign Office slowly came around to her terms, introducing new complications, from the Soviet point of view, with each professed "concession." The Germans had presented a more detailed version of their views to Mikoyan on July 10. The Russians recalled their trade representative in Berlin, Barbarin, for detailed instructions and on July 18, the day after Molotov requested a definite answer from Britain and France on military negotiations, Barbarin called on Schnurre and stated that he was authorized to discuss mutual concessions and, if possible, to conclude and sign a trade agreement in Berlin. On July 21 Schnurre agreed to the negotiations.[154] Now the Germans began cautiously sounding out the Russians on the prospect for a political pact. On July 26, Schnurre dined with Astakhov and Barbarin and brought up political matters, including the suggestion of a nonaggression pact. Astakhov seemed skeptical and indicated that Russian and German vital interests in the Balkans and Rumania were in conflict. On July 29 Weizsacker informed Schulenburg of Schnurre's conversation and instructed the ambassador to sound out Molotov's reaction if he saw "an opportunity of arranging a further conversation." [155] On August 2, Schnurre wrote Schulenburg that "politically, the problem of Russia is being dealt with here with *extreme urgency.*" [156] As-

153. Ibid., pp. 375–77.
154. McSherry, pp. 161–62.
155. DGFP, 6: 1015–16.
156. Ibid., pp. 1047–48.

takhov was contacted by Ribbentrop on the evening of August 2 and by Schnurre on the afternoon of the 3rd. Astakhov told Schnurre that the Soviet Government regarded an economic treaty as a first stage in achieving the goal of improved relations, but that Molotov still wanted a more specific expression of the wishes of the German Government.[157] Schulenburg met with Molotov on August 3 and reported his impression that while the Soviet Government was becoming more receptive to the idea of a rapprochement, "the old mistrust of Germany persists." "My general impression is that the Soviet Government are at present determined to conclude an agreement with Britain and France if they fulfill all Soviet wishes," the ambassador wrote to Ribbentrop. "It will, nevertheless, require considerable effort on our part to cause a reversal in the Soviet Government's course." [158] In the meantime, fighting with Japan had been renewed in May 1939 and was still raging on; the fighting was on a scale far greater than mere border clashes, involving battles with armor and aircraft, and Stalin was confronted with the serious threat that Japan, with Germany's aid, would declare war on Russia.[159]

Stalin was still not willing to foreclose any option. With Britain and France so reluctant to agree to the final terms that Moscow felt essential for protection in the widest variety of foreseeable contingencies, and with war with Japan threatening in the East, Stalin could not risk being isolated in the event that Germany struck Poland, as she now seriously threatened to do. Churchill had pointed out Russia's "vital need," should Germany attack Poland, "to hold the deployment positions of the German armies as far to the west as possible so as to give the Russians more time for assembling their forces from all parts of their immense empire. . . . They must be in occupation of the Baltic States and a large part of Poland by force or fraud before they were attacked." [160] As late as the middle of August, Stalin was uncertain as to whether Hitler would agree to terms that would

157. Ibid., pp. 1051–52.
158. Ibid., pp. 1059–62.
159. Rubinstein, p. 115; Taylor, p. 241.
160. Churchill, pp. 393–94.

make it worthwhile for Russia to enter into a nonaggression pact with Germany. Hence, the alternative of an alliance with Britain and France was still a very important objective of Stalin's foreign policy, provided it could fulfill everything Moscow considered essential. Now was the time to find out how serious London and Paris were with respect to a military alliance with Moscow. Now, writes Ulam, the Russians "wanted to have the most precise information of what the West would and could do for them in case the German gambit failed and they found themselves in war." [161]

On July 21 Halifax responded to Seeds's request of three days earlier for further instructions in the light of Molotov's insistence that Britain and France give official replies on the issue of a simultaneous political and military agreement. He stated that the British government was "prepared . . . to agree to the simultaneous entry into force" of the two agreements, but that approval of immediate military conversations should be given only "in the last resort," after all efforts had failed to secure Russian approval of a version of Article I acceptable to the British. On the matter of indirect aggression, Halifax stated that the Soviet definition was still unacceptable because the British "may be placed in position of becoming accessories to interference in the internal affairs of other States." [162]

When Molotov, Seeds, and Naggier met next, on July 23, Seeds repeated his Government's agreement to the principle that the military and political agreements enter into force at the same time, and expressed his hope that the Soviet Government would recognize that the definition of indirect aggression "was a question of principle for us." This plea from a representative of the Government that, less than a year before, had forced a free country to surrender its independence and submit to German demands, must have been hard for Molotov to swallow. The British doubtless had legitimate fears, as often voiced by Halifax, that a guarantee against indirect aggression as defined by the

161. Ulam, p. 275.
162. DBFP, 6: 427–29.

Soviets might have the effect of driving many of the guaranteed States into closer relationships with Germany. At any rate, Molotov stated that he did not think the problem of a definition "would raise insuperable difficulties" and he was confident that a satisfactory formula could be found. Naggier expressed his agreement with the British position, although in private he told Seeds that he felt the Soviet definition of indirect aggression "could be accepted." [163] Seeds himself seemed to have confidence in Molotov's assurance that a solution could be found, and he pointed out to Halifax that "it must be remembered in [Molotov's] favor that he dropped at once his original most objectionable formula ('coup d'etat and reversal of policy') when I objected to it under instructions on July 8." [164] However, at this point in the negotiations, the definition was a less important concern to the Russians than the immediate opening of military staff talks. Now Molotov repeated the question he had posed on July 17: would the British and French Governments consent to the start of military negotiations before the details of the political agreement had been thrashed out? As before, the two ambassadors said they would have to contact their governments before responding.[165]

Halifax wired Seeds on July 25 that the British Government was prepared to agree to the "immediate initiation of military conversations at Moscow without waiting for the final agreement on Article I." [166] This position was conveyed to Molotov on July 27 by Seeds and Naggier.[167]

I have already examined Soviet foreign policy through early August in the context of these negotiations. It is now necessary to examine British foreign policy in the same period to understand British objectives in negotiating an agreement with Russia.

British policy toward Germany after March 1939 cannot be

163. Ibid., p. 450.
164. Ibid., pp. 460–61.
165. Ibid., pp. 456–60.
166. Ibid., p. 478.
167. Ibid., p. 521.

properly described as an abandonment of appeasement. As I explained earlier in this chapter, the German aggressions of March 15–17 cast British appeasement policy into a new mold, and the events of the four months following March drew the British further along the basic lines adopted in March. A cornerstone of British policy was the acceleration of the armaments program, for the reasons that (1) the British public and Chamberlain's political opposition would tolerate nothing less now, (2) Britain could no longer afford to be in a position where it could not resist unreasonable demands from Hitler, and (3) the Chamberlain cabinet was finally persuaded that force and power were what Hitler understood. Now Hitler was pressing his demands against Poland for the free city of Danzig; he followed the basic contours of his previous aggressions, justifying his policy on the basis of the repressed German minorities in the area and applying all forms of pressure and threats. The British and French were apparently determined, for a variety of reasons, to fight Hitler if he went to war over Danzig. However, at the heart of British policy was the inability to conceive of Hitler's going to war over Danzig; Chamberlain still held to his position, stated in March, that "I never accept the view that war is inevitable." [168] Now, as Chamberlain and his followers in the Government saw things, the best way to prevent war was to relentlessly make the price of war for Hitler higher and higher, and hold open the possibility that a peaceful settlement would be possible if Hitler would give some demonstration of his intention not to make war. Of course, as Hitler pressed his demands, the chances that he would give evidence of peaceful intentions grew slimmer and slimmer. The British Government recognized this, but were always highly sensitive to any gesture or indication by Germany that a peaceful solution could be worked out.

It was on May 24, 1939, that Halifax told Ambassador Ken-

168. Feiling, p. 401.

nedy that the British and French Governments had decided on the necessity of meeting the Russian insistence on an agreement stipulating mutual obligations. During this conversation Halifax also informed Kennedy about a very interesting talk he had had with German Ambassador Dirksen, in private, "away from the Foreign Office." Dirksen told Halifax that Hitler would not make war if he had to fight France, England, Turkey, Poland, Russia, and possibly the United States. "Halifax thought it very strange that Dirksen should include Russia," because at the time the British-French negotiations with Russia were going so poorly. Evidently, Dirksen was attempting to warn Halifax that Hitler might not be deterred from war unless the Anglo-French-Soviet negotiations resulted in an alliance. Halifax's subsequent actions indicated that the British were very much interested in keeping the negotiations going, although the evidence does not permit the assumption that they had an equal interest in bringing the negotiations to a successful conclusion. As Halifax told Kennedy in relating his meeting with the German Ambassador, he

> suggested to Dirksen that word be got to Hitler that if he would make a speech or a gesture of some kind that he did not want war and that he was hoping for peace and that while Danzig was an irritant it could probably be worked out, regardless of what popular opinion in [Britain] might be, Halifax assured Dirksen that officially England would welcome the statement and would so reply.
>
> Halifax in the meantime is preparing a speech which he is going to give before some organization, trying to hold the door open for economic discussion with Hitler and has suggested that he will let Dirksen see the speech before he delivers it to see if any suggestions might be made.[169]

A month later, Halifax had another conversation with Kennedy in which he indicated that Britain was anxious for some sign from Hitler, but frustrated that no response from Hitler was forthcoming. Kennedy wrote:

169. FRUS (1939), 1: 260.

Halifax feels that the German situation is certainly very restless at the minute but believes that Danzig can be settled between Poland and Germany if Hitler wants it settled; they can get no assurances from him, however, that he wants to do anything with England.[170]

Thus, concerned and perplexed that his private conversation with Dirksen had produced no results, Halifax attempted to push the door to cooperation with Hitler a bit farther open in a speech at Catham House on June 29. Halifax had told Kennedy of his intention to make such a speech more than a month before. Now, at Catham House, Halifax repeated in explicit terms his Government's determination to resist aggression, and he pointed to Britain's greatly expanded military strength. However, he had another point to stress:

British policy rests on twin foundations of purpose. One is determination to resist force. The other is our recognition of the world's desire to get on with the constructive work of building peace. If we could once be satisfied that the intentions of others were the same as our own, and that we all really wanted peaceful solutions—then, I say here definitely, we could discuss the problems that are today causing the world anxiety. In such a new atmosphere we could examine the colonial problem, the problem of raw materials, trade barriers, the issue of *Lebensraum* ["living space"], the limitation of armaments, and any other issue that affects the lives of all European citizens.

But this is not the position which we face today.[171]

Obviously, this speech was a plea that "the position . . . we face today" be changed, that is, that Germany do something to demonstrate its peaceful intentions, whereupon Britain would be willing to negotiate a long-range, comprehensive agreement. Halifax also said in this speech that the view of his Government was that "deeds, not words, are necessary" on Germany's part.

170. Ibid., p. 276.
171. Halifax Speeches, p. 296.

A week later, on July 5, Halifax told Kennedy that he was " of the belief that England's appearing stronger all the time is having an effect in Germany." [172]

One of the first indications of Germany's receptiveness to a peaceful settlement of her claims came on July 6 when Dr. Erich Kordt, Ribbentrop's private secretary, requested a meeting with Adrian Holman, the British chargé in Berlin. Kordt said that "it was absolutely necessary to find a solution" to the Danzig problem, but that it was also "unthinkable that a world war could be waged on such an issue." Kordt cautioned Holman

> that we should not allow ourselves to be carried away by a fit of nerves, and that it was all important that His Majesty's Government should, as they had a perfect right, put pressure on the Poles to take no offensive action against Danzig. If this could be achieved, he could assure me privately and confidentially that in six months' time there would be a completely altered situation in Germany, which would open the road to peace and understanding.[173]

On July 10, Neville Henderson called on Bonnet in Paris, and discussed the issue of Danzig. Henderson felt "that the next two months would be decisive one way or the other," but that, in his opinion, the British "display of force had intimidated" Hitler, as revealed by the fact that Hitler had failed to take decisive action against Danzig. Then, pointing out that "Mussolini's intervention [at Munich] had been *the* decisive factor for peace," Henderson said that Mussolini was the "one man in Europe who might play a decisive role if the [current] crisis became really acute." He thus "deplored" France's hesitation to begin conversations with the Italian Government.[174] Furthermore, on July 12, Henderson wrote to Halifax that "if there is to be a change for the better, then we must try to get away from all this nervous tension. I am going to work to that end, in Berlin.

172. FRUS (1939), 1: 283.
173. DBFP, 6: 285–87.
174. Ibid., pp. 329–32.

. . . In my opinion there has been enough talking about Danzig. . . . I have no chance of succeeding unless our Russian negotiations terminate one way or the other quickly." [175] What Henderson wanted was a quieting down of all the stormy voices in Britain threatening war if Germany took unilateral action in Danzig. The Germans knew the British position, Henderson argued; now the decision for war was up to them, and they would be inclined toward a peaceful solution only if Britain showed cool force and did not stir the air with endless threats of war.

Halifax wrote to Henderson on July 13 and expressed his agreement with each of the Ambassador's points. "I am very glad you had a good talk to Bonnet and said what you did. The P.M. is writing to Phipps today to arm him with something on which to approach Daladier as regards the possibility of Franco-Italian talks." In the same letter Halifax wrote, "I agree with you that the less said the better." Chamberlain, he wrote, had "exhorted members of the Cabinet yesterday to be as economical in their references to foreign affairs as the state of public opinion here would permit." Meanwhile, as a show of force, Chamberlain would announce "extended fleet exercises," which "may have a useful effect." [176]

On the same day, as Halifax indicated, Chamberlain wrote to Daladier through Phipps. He asked that France "reconsider the Franco-Italian position." In his arguments, he virtually quoted from Henderson's advice:

> Any step of this nature that you might feel able to take would probably increase the Italian ability or disposition to exercise a restraining influence in regard to the situation in Danzig which may otherwise at any time reach an acute stage. In this connection I feel that Mussolini is the one man who can influence Hitler to keep the peace.

In justifying this move, Chamberlain made reference to the cur-

175. Ibid., pp. 713–14.
176. Ibid., p. 353.

rent untenable state of affairs in Europe and the need to find a peaceful solution:

> The commitments into which France and Great Britain have entered and the agreements which will embody them have created a situation in which some sort of precarious balance of power exists. But that position cannot be permanently maintained and if a real peace is to be established we must make some positive efforts of a constructive character to ease the tension and restore confidence in Europe.[177]

By July 20, there had been numerous indications that Hitler might be willing to seek a peaceful solution to the Danzig problem, and these indications, attributed to Britain's show of force, were summarized in a Foreign Office memorandum of July 20.[178] On July 20 Chamberlain told Kennedy he thought that "England's movements, beginning with conscription and now the calling up of reserves in the navy, have made a definite impression on Hitler and may cause him to change his mind about taking a gamble on a world war. He is not joyful over the prospects."[179] On the same day, the British chargé in Danzig wired Halifax that "it is important that atmosphere should not be prejudiced by violent newspaper comment and I therefore submit that a hint in this sense might be given to the British press."[180] Henderson immediately wrote Halifax strongly recommending the adoption of this "useful suggestion." "Our resolute determination to resist aggression by force is not weakened by expression of a desire to create an atmosphere in which negotiations may again become possible."[181] On July 21, Halifax wired the British chargé in Warsaw:

> I am most anxious that this tentative move from the German side should not be compromised by publicity or by any

177. Ibid., pp. 350–52.
178. Ibid., pp. 411–13.
179. FRUS (1939), 1: 288.
180. DBFP, 6: 401.
181. Ibid., p. 432.

disinclination on part of Polish Government to discuss in
friendly and reasonable spirit [a settlement]. . . .

There is some reason to think that German policy is now
to work for a detente in the Danzig question. This, if confirmed, may be held to be the first fruit of firm attitude
adopted by His Majesty's Government and French and Polish
Governments. It is nevertheless essential not to destroy possibility of better atmosphere at outset and I trust that more care
than ever will be taken on Polish side to avoid provocation
in any sphere and to restrain press.[182]

On the same day, Halifax wrote Henderson in somewhat
different terms. He admitted that he felt "pretty certain" that
conditions for the peaceful settlement of the Danzig question
"do not in fact prevail at this moment, and that we have to work
for their re-creation." Furthermore:

> I should like nothing better, if it were possible, than to
> restrict press polemics, but as you know that is not possible,
> and all we can with some assurance say to ourselves and the
> Germans is that if they could make a practical contribution
> to the lowering of the temperature, this question would gradu-
> ally tend to settle itself. . . .
> It may be that if the Danzig situation can be developed
> favourably, this may open the door to other things, but in the
> meanwhile I think that our line must continue to be a stiff
> one, while letting it be known, on the lines of my Catham
> House speech, that whenever the German Government gave
> concrete evidence of their willingness to forswear force, we
> should be willing to meet them half-way.[183]

At this time, the British made an unofficial feeler to the Germans for renewed negotiations leading toward a general settlement. As Dirksen wrote in the review of his Ambassadorship in
London, "in the middle of July, Anglo-German relations became
a little more tranquil" and the atmosphere in Danzig "calmer."
Throughout the early summer of 1939 Dirksen had been inform-
ing his government that the inflamed state of British public

182. Ibid., pp. 432–33.
183. Ibid., pp. 441–42.

opinion did not mean that the country "is now irrevocably heading for war." On July 10 he wrote that "within the Cabinet, and in a small but influential group of politicians, efforts are being made to replace the negative policy of an encirclement front by a constructive policy towards Germany." [184] Two weeks later he wrote that "the few really decisive statesmen in Britain have considered and put into more concrete form the lines of thought" of a "constructive" policy toward Germany.[185] In this atmosphere, Dirksen later recalled, the "constructive trends in the British Government—which . . . sought to reach agreement with Germany by way of negotiation—began to shape into positive action. For this purpose Staatsrat Wohlthat was applied to." Wohlthat, special economic commissioner for the Four-Year Plan, was in London for whaling negotiations in July, and "had good relations with" Sir Horace Wilson, one of Chamberlain's closest advisers, and Sir R. S. Hudson, Secretary of the Department of Overseas Trade.[186] Wohlthat met with Wilson on July 18 and 21, and with Hudson on the 20th. Wohlthat's minutes of his meeting with these two men [187] differ from their version of the conversations [188] with respect to who initiated the talks and the extent of British negotiating offers expressed during the talks; also, Wilson does not recall having met with Wohlthat on July 21. It seems unlikely that Wohlthat would have fabricated many elements of what he reported to his government, including the text of a memorandum presented by Wilson containing the British position on possible concessions to be made to Germany in the event of negotiations. Likewise, it seems plausible that Wilson and Hudson might have been inclined to leave a record that would have enabled them to deny that such offers had been made to the Germans. Wilson himself indirectly confirmed the accuracy of Wohlthat's minutes. Wilson met with Dirksen on

184. DGFP, 6: 892–93.
185. Ibid., p. 969.
186. Dirksen Papers, pp. 182–83.
187. DGFP, 6, No. 716
188. DBFP, 6, Nos. 354, 370.

August 3, at which time he was impressed by Dirksen's "knowledge . . . of Wohlthat's conversations here," the details of which Dirksen had learned from messages from Berlin based on Wohlthat's "written report." [189] Nevertheless, there are enough points of agreement between the written recollections of each side to enable the historian to get a good sense of what transpired in the discussions.

According to Wilson, Wohlthat brought up the point that negotiations between the two countries should be resumed:

> He did not press this point, and I then asked him whether he had done anything to make up what, at the earlier conversation [in June], he called the "frame-work" which, as he had said before, would have to be wide enough in scope to include a sufficient number of topics to make it acceptable as a whole to both countries. . . . It seemed to me that, if it was his view that anything could be done, it would be necessary for him to put the points down in simple language. I did not press him to do this, as I was most anxious to maintain the position that I had adopted in the June conversation, namely, that . . . the initiative must come from the German side. I said that he would find in the Prime Minister's speeches and in Lord Halifax's recent speech plenty of material to enable him to understand the British position. He would find, for example, that, while it had been made abundantly clear what preparations we had made to carry out our undertakings, there was still an opportunity for co-operation . . . so soon as conditions had been created that would make that co-operation feasible.[190]

This was Wilson's way of saying that he had invited Germany to submit proposals for comprehensive negotiations, and that his government was ready to negotiate pending a concrete sign from Hitler that he did not intend to make war.

Wohlthat's minute of the conversation is similar to Wilson's in many respects, including mention of Wilson's warnings about the advanced state of British armaments and request "for a statement of points which, in the Führer's view, should be discussed

189. Ibid., p. 580.
190. Ibid., p. 391.

by both Governments." However, Wohlthat describes in minute detail an overture by Wilson never mentioned in Wilson's account. Wohlthat writes that Wilson had "prepared a memorandum" that contained an elaboration of the British view "of the points which would have to be dealt with between the German and British Governments." Perhaps open to suspicion is Wohlthat's apparent assumption that this memorandum was "approved by Neville Chamberlain." The memorandum contained proposals for a nonaggression pact by which Britain could rid herself of her newly assumed obligations in Eastern Europe, an agreement on the limitations of armaments, and a comprehensive economic agreement. Dirksen's report of a conversation with Wilson on August 3 provides some corroboration for Wohlthat's account of Wilson's offer to negotiate. Wohlthat noted Wilson's concern "that the conversation must be held in secret." [191] Dirksen, in his report of the August 3 conversation, describes Wilson's account to him of the meeting with Wohlthat and confirms Wilson's concern for secrecy: "Wilson expatiated at length on the great risk Chamberlain would incur by starting confidential negotiations with the German Government. If anything about them were to leak out there would be a great scandal, and Chamberlain would probably be forced to resign." [192] Dirksen reports that Wilson felt the conversation with Wohlthat had "made known to the German Government [Britain's] readiness to negotiate." Wilson confirmed that this was "an official British feeler, to which a German reply was now expected." [193]

For his part, Hudson readily admitted that he had told Wohlthat "that, given the necessary preliminary of a solution of the political question, it ought not to be impossible to work out some form of economic and industrial collaboration between" England, Germany, and the United States. He said that his Government recognized southeastern Europe "as falling within the natural economic sphere of Germany and we had no objec-

191. DGFP, 6: 797.
192. Dirksen Papers, p. 120.
193. Ibid., p. 124.

tion to her developing her position in that market, provided we were assured of a reasonable share." Hudson also said, in what he described as a personal capacity, that "if Hitler was prepared to disarm and to accept adequate safeguards against rearming the possibility was opened up of establishing Germany on a strong economic basis. . . . Wohlthat said he thoroughly agreed." [194]

On July 23 and 24, the British press carried leaked stories about Wohlthat's conversation with Hudson, including mention of a "peace plan" offered by the British, providing for disarmament, a colonial settlement, and a large loan to Germany. This news had a sensational effect all over Europe. German papers immediately gave "full publicity" to and quoted large excerpts from the stories that appeared in the British press.[195] In Italy, messages from London and Berlin gave "the greatest prominence" to the disclosure.[196] The Polish press gave "great prominence" to the allegations concerning the Hudson-Wohlthat meeting.[197] As of July 26, "the uneasiness caused in France by the conversations with Herr Wohlthat has by no means died down." Among French analysts the "general conclusion is that such conversations . . . must inevitably cause doubt as to Great Britain's attitude among her friends . . . there is an under-current of disturbance that such discussions . . . should have taken place in the capital of one of the members of the peace front without the previous knowledge of the Governments of France or the other participating countries." [198]

One can imagine the reaction to this leak in the Kremlin! On the surface, one might say that all that the Russians would be justified in asserting was that "two can play at the same game"—coming to terms with Germany by means of economic negotiations that could lead to further comprehensive agree-

194. DBFP, 6: 407–10.
195. Ibid., pp. 465, 481.
196. Ibid., p. 466.
197. Ibid., p. 482.
198. Ibid., p. 495.

ments. This view, however, is not justified by the evidence, for there was a fundamental difference in the nature and aims of the British and the Soviet approaches to Hitler. The Russians recognized that they were threatened by Hitler's very existence as the leader of Germany; they sought an alliance with Britain and France to enable them to take strong and definite measures to contain Hitler, enhance their untenable defensive position against him, and assemble sufficient force to assure his defeat if he made war; but this was something on which they could not depend because of the attitudes of the British and French Governments. Therefore they kept the door open to an agreement with Hitler that would give them temporary protection against attack, a chance to consolidate their defensive position both militarily and strategically, and the prospect that when they eventually did fight Hitler, he would be exhausted from war in the West. In their approaches to Hitler, they never deviated from the demand that *all* their terms be met. The British, on the other hand, entered into negotiations with Russia only because they desired a unilateral declaration to "steady" the European situation and make their long-sought goal of a *permanent* understanding with Hitler once more feasible. As the clouds over Europe grew darker, the British attached more importance to an agreement with Russia not as an effective preparation for an actual war, but as a means of raising the stakes for Hitler, to deter him from making war. Although the British leaders certainly recognized the delicacy of the situation, at the heart of their policy, including that of negotiating with the Russians, was the belief that at some point they would have to come to terms with Hitler. They offered to meet Hitler "half way" if he would show some sign of peaceful intentions.

This basic element of British policy was very carefully outlined on July 26 in a letter from Henderson to Halifax. Henderson described his admiration for Hitler based on what the German leader had achieved, but he did not approve of Hitler's methods or "the gangsters and brigands who surround him." But Henderson attempted to be entirely realistic:

While regimes are not permanent, Germany is; and the reality of the new Great Germany has got to be understood and faced. It may be fated that Britain must again fight Germany, yet it is a consummation devoutly to be avoided if it can be humanly possible to do so. There can be no peace in Europe until Germany and Britain discover some basis of mutual existence. The sooner that basis can be found the better, since another war is far less likely to provide it. . . .

So far as Britain is concerned an understanding with Germany must comprise two essential admissions: firstly, that of full and equal collaboration with Germany in settling world problems. . . ; and secondly that of Germany's paramount economic importance in Central and Eastern Europe. . . .

Peace is Britain's chief interest, and I cannot imagine that she would wish to deny a really peacefully inclined Germany these two preliminary and axiomatic admissions. The stumbling block is, of course, the exaggerated ambitions and enthusiasms of a Germany in the first flush of the Nazi revolution and of her unity and recovered national prestige. Excess is unfortunately and tragically inherent in revolutions. . . .

It is not impossible that Hitler may consider it more prudent, having achieved so much, not to start a war for what remains. He may well regard it as preferable to obtain somewhat less than his full desiderata by negotiation rather than risk the whole of his winnings at one blow. Much may depend in this respect on the attitude of His Majesty's Government: and not only on their firmness, but also on their understanding of the reality of Great Germany. Both are essential.[199]

The same sympathy was not to be found in regard to another great power, formed out of a revolution and ruled by an excessive dictator who had made great strides for his country and who had claims to stake in Europe. This dictator had not committed aggression in Europe but had opposed it; this dictator did not scorn an attempt to reach an agreement with Britain and France on an equal basis, but rather invited such an agreement.

Halifax responded to Henderson's letter on July 28 with the apology that he did not have time to write at length. He repeated his determination to keep public speeches warning Germany at a

199. Ibid., pp. 497–501.

minimum, because such speeches would weaken the impression of strength and make it "more difficult for reason to assert itself in other quarters." He concluded, "I cannot help feeling that the one essential thing to do, without provocation or advertisement, is to get it into Hitler's head that further forceful acts on his part will mean war. Once he has got this firmly in mind, may it not be that he might be willing to try and use other and more peaceful methods?" [200]

Chamberlain fully agreed with this policy. On July 30 he wrote that Britain must convince Germany

> that the chances of winning a war without getting thoroughly exhausted in the process are too remote to make it worthwhile. But the corollary to that must be that she has a chance of getting fair and reasonable consideration from us and others, if she will give up the idea that she can force it from us, and convince us that she has given it up.

Chamberlain's biographer writes, "But the time for this, he added, had not yet come; nor, we may think, was it likely to be speeded by a break-down in the Anglo-Russian negotiation." [201]

On August 2, Theo Kordt, chargé at the German embassy in London, requested a meeting with "some authoritative person" before reporting to Berlin. At Chamberlain's instruction, a meeting between Kordt and Sir Horace Wilson was arranged for the following day. However, Kordt did not attend the meeting, and in his place the German ambassador, Dirksen, appeared.[202] Wilson's [203] and Dirksen's [204] accounts of their lengthy conversation are remarkably similar, with the major exception of their version of who initiated the meeting (each points to the other) and Wilson's omission of his explanation, recorded by Dirksen, of why Anglo-German negotiations must be conducted

200. Ibid., pp. 529–30.
201. Feiling, pp. 409–10.
202. DBFP, 6: 580.
203. Ibid., No. 533.
204. Dirksen Papers, No. 24.

in secrecy. Wilson admits expressing his Government's readiness to negotiate on the condition that Hitler make some positive move, or at least refrain from taking any steps to worsen the situation. He also confirms something that Wohlthat reported him as saying on July 18, that "if it was once made clear by the German Government that there was henceforth to be no aggression on their part, the policy of guarantees to potential victims ipso facto became inoperative." [205] Wilson, as both parties report, expressed a great interest in finding some gesture, to be made by Hitler and acceptable to both sides, to aid the "restoration of confidence." Dirksen quotes Wilson as saying that "it would be a severe disappointment to the British side if we did not take up the thread [spun by Wohlthat's visit]. In that case there would be nothing left but to drive to disaster." [206] Wilson left Dirksen with three questions to ponder, the substance of which is recorded almost identically by both men: (1) What instructions has Hitler given as to the follow-up of the Wohlthat report, (2) will Hitler not aggravate the situation in the next few weeks, and (3) if an agenda for negotiations is worked out, what will Hitler do to create a suitable atmosphere in which the negotiations could proceed? [207]

On August 9, Dirksen, before going on leave, met with Halifax. The accounts of the meeting rendered by each participant are essentially the same, with the exception that Dirksen presents Halifax's views of possible negotiations with Germany in more detail. Halifax admits that he told the German Ambassador that the British public was not irreversibly committed to war, but rather that public opinion and the British Government awaited a gesture from Hitler that would help to restore the confidence that Hitler himself had shattered. The restoration "would necessarily take time," Halifax said, assuring Dirksen "as I had assured him in May, that, if Herr Hitler would make any real effort in this

205. DBFP, 6: 580.
206. Dirksen Papers, p. 123.
207. Ibid., pp. 123–24; DBFP, 6: 582.

direction, we would certainly respond from this side and in this way, provided this was, in fact, his intention, we might look to an improvement in confidence being gradually effected." [208] Dirksen adds that Halifax said "he was certain that once the ice were broken, the British side would go very far to reach an adjustment with Germany . . . it was . . . certain that a period of calm making for the pacification of public opinion would create an entirely different picture" from the one that currently existed. "The British Government keenly desired that this should come about." [209]

These British efforts were to no avail. Rather than make the slightest attempt to temper the situation, Hitler continued to press his demands and make military preparations for war.[210]

Halifax had given his approval on July 25 to the immediate commencement of military staff talks in Moscow. In light of the above discussion of British policy, there would seem to be little doubt that the principal British concern in agreeing to start these talks was that they would prevent the negotiations from breaking down and would provide Hitler with a further demonstration of the strength of the Anglo-French position and the imminence of an alliance with Russia. Indeed, in recommending approval of the military negotiations to Halifax, Seeds argued that "to begin with them now would give a healthy shock to the Axis Powers and a fillip to our friends while they might be prolonged sufficiently to tide over the next dangerous few months." [211] Halifax was apparently in accord with the view that Britain should stall the military talks. In the top secret instructions to the British Military Mission to Moscow, headed by Admiral Drax, the Foreign Office wrote that the only reason Britain agreed to the talks was to prevent the breakdown of the political negotiations; however, the delegation was instructed as follows:

208. DBFP, 6: 647–48.
209. Dirksen Papers, pp. 126–31.
210. DBFP, 6, Nos. 592, 614, 660.
211. Ibid., p. 461.

Until such time as the political agreement is concluded, the Delegation should therefore go very slowly with the conversations, watching the progress of the political negotiations and keeping in very close touch with His Majesty's Ambassador.[212]

The British seemed to spare no effort to let the Russians know that they were not serious about the military negotiations. Within the period of a month, during which the British knew that the Russians were awaiting an answer on the question of military negotiations, Seeds put off a settlement of the question on four occasions by claiming that he had to check back with his government for further instructions. Then, on July 24, in response to a hint from Molotov that the British were stalling by making military negotiations dependent on the settlement of the entire political agreement, Seeds assured the Russians that the British Government "had no intention of wasting time." [213] Yet, the Anglo-French military delegations, dispatched on July 31, traveled by ship to Leningrad, and then by train to Moscow, taking a total of eleven days in traveling time. The first meeting of delegates took place on August 12. The Soviet and French delegates each produced a document from their respective governments authorizing them to negotiate a military agreement. The British, however, had no written credentials! Drax wired home for written authority to negotiate: "Please send by air mail." [214] Apparently airplanes were in short supply for dealings with the Russians; Drax's credentials arrived and were presented on August 18. Voroshilov, Soviet Commissar for Defense and head of the Russian delegation at the talks, had at once "suggested that the conversations should continue while waiting for the credentials." [215]

On the following morning, August 13, Seeds wired Halifax with an apparent change of heart from his previous suggestion

212. Ibid., p. 763.
213. Ibid., p. 458.
214. Ibid., p. 674.
215. Ibid.

that the military talks be drawn out. Now, with the concurrence of Naggier, Seeds felt that the Russians "will probably evade coming to any agreement with us on these political points, until [they have] reason to believe that military talks have at least made very considerable progress." In this context, Seeds now feared that if the British military delegation followed its instruction to draw out the talks, "Russian fears that we are not in earnest" would tend to be confirmed. Thus Seeds requested immediate information as to whether his Government still wanted to stall the military talks pending agreement on the "indirect aggression" problem. He warned that "all indications so far go to show that Soviet military negotiators are really out for business." [216] On August 15, Halifax agreed to reverse the instructions.

At the close of the first negotiating session on August 13, Voroshilov observed that, before discussing Soviet military plans at the next meeting, he would want to know what action the British and French staffs felt Russia should take in the event of a German attack because Soviet forces would have to be based on the territory of other States in order to fight Germany.[217] The following morning Voroshilov repeated his question and, in this connection, asked specifically if Russian troops could cross Polish and Rumanian territory to fight Germany. The British and French delegates tried to avoid any commitment, but Voroshilov insisted that without an unequivocal answer, further discussion would be useless. Drax, speaking for the British and French, offered to have the allied missions ask their governments to take the issue up with Warsaw and Bucharest. Voroshilov accepted the offer and submitted detailed written questions to be asked concerning the passage of troops. Although he maintained that "without a solution to this question . . . the Soviet Military Mission cannot recommend to its Government to take part in an enterprise so obviously doomed to failure," he still considered it possible for the negotiations to proceed pending an

216. Ibid., pp. 682–83.
217. Ibid., 6: 565–70.

expeditious reply.[218] During the discussions on August 17, Voroshilov announced that if an answer on the Polish and Rumanian question was not received by the next morning, the meetings would have to be suspended. At Drax's urging, Voroshilov agreed to postpone his deadline until August 21.[219] The following morning the talks were officially suspended pending a reply on the troop passage issue. Drax formally stated that the British and French could not take responsibility for the delay in the talks and implied that Moscow acted in bad faith by inviting the missions while all along intending "to put to them at once difficult political questions . . . requir[ing] reference to our Governments." Voroshilov took the opposite view, stating that he could not imagine how Britain and France, in dispatching missions to arrange a military convention, "could not have given them some directives on such an elementary matter as the passage of Soviet armed forces against" German troops "on the territory of Poland and Rumania, with which countries France and Britain have corresponding military and political agreements." [220]

All other considerations aside, Voroshilov's point was quite valid. "Good sense was on the side of the Russians," writes Fontaine.[221] As another historian has commented, even if complete agreement between Russia and the Western Powers has been reached, "the question would still remain what form her action should take while Poland and Rumania adhered to their refusal to allow her troops to enter their territory; and surely Russia, before undertaking to fight, was justified in asking where, how, and in what circumstances she would have to do so." [222] Furthermore, Seeds and Naggier agreed that "Soviet negotiators are justified in putting on Great Britain and France the onus of approaching those countries." [223] However, Britain was deter-

218. Ibid., pp. 570–75.
219. Ibid., pp. 584–89.
220. Ibid., pp. 589–93.
221. Fontaine, p. 115.
222. Namier, pp. 204–5.
223. DBFP, 7: 1–2.

mined to delay the whole issue. Ideally, Seeds and Halifax thought in terms of securing prior Soviet agreement that the contingency of an attack on Poland would be excluded from the military discussions.[224] Halifax wired Seeds on July 25 that "imminence of military conversations makes it important that position of Poland should be cleared up," yet the only suggestions he could offer do not bespeak a serious approach toward the military talks. To Halifax, "clearing up" the Polish (and Rumanian) issue involved not preparing for contingencies of war, but rather how to evade the issue in negotiation: "I shall be grateful to have your views as to whether it would be best now to tell M. Molotov frankly that we propose the contingency of Polish aggression should be excluded from scope of Staff conversations or when the time comes for our military representatives to say that they are not instructed to discuss this contingency." [225] In his response of July 26, Seeds indicated that it would not be wise to raise the issue beforehand with Molotov, but that it would also be difficult to exclude the contingency from discussion at the staff meetings. Seeds tried to play down the matter as one of many issues that could cause a "hitch in military conversations." [226] Finally, the British instructed their military delegation that "if the Russians propose that the British and French Governments should communicate to the Polish, Rumanian or Baltic States proposals involving co-operation with the Soviet Government for General Staff, the Delegation should not commit themselves but refer home." [227]

Thus the British did indeed anticipate that the Russians would inevitably raise the issue of military actions with respect to Poland and Rumania, and it was the British, not the Russians, who were guilty of bad faith in agreeing to the staff talks fully knowing that they were unprepared to negotiate on a central issue. On August 20 and 21 the French, with British approval,

224. Ibid., 6: 112, 129.
225. Ibid., pp. 476–77.
226. Ibid., pp. 493–94.
227. Ibid., p. 764.

made a desperate, last-ditch effort to force Warsaw into accepting Soviet military assistance. On the 20th, Naggier and the head of the French Military Mission wired Paris that "M. Beck's objections should not be taken altogether literally, and that perhaps he merely wishes not to know anything about the matter"; they urged an affirmative reply to the principle of the right of passage of Soviet troops through Poland. On the 21st Bonnet approved this request, and Daladier sent instructions to the military mission to give Poland's advance approval and sign the best agreement they could get. In 1946, Daladier recalled that on the morning of the 21st he summoned the Polish Ambassador in Paris to inform him that France intended to sign with Russia and that if Poland persisted in her negative attitude, "France would be compelled to reconsider her treaty of alliance." (The Polish Ambassador later denied that such an ultimatum was ever delivered.) [228]

These efforts were superfluous, for on August 23, Russia signed a nonaggression pact with Germany. The events directly leading to this agreement are worthy of consideration. I have already described the resumption of German-Soviet trade talks at the end of July and the corresponding eagerness in Berlin to reach an agreement with Russia. On August 5 Molotov sent word to Schnurre, in response to the latter's inquiries, that Moscow was prepared to continue the trade negotiations and considered the conclusion of a trade agreement as the first step in improving relations. However, when Schnurre met with Astakhov, he expressed his regret at Moscow's failure to put forth precise points of interest, thus inhibiting concrete discussion. Berlin, he indicated, was particularly interested in learning Soviet intentions toward Poland and the impending staff talks with England and France. Astakhov was noncommittal and stated that it was still too early to settle the problem of Poland.[229] At this point, the Anglo-French military delegation had just arrived in Leningrad, on their way to Moscow. On the morning

228. McSherry, p. 223; Thorne, p. 147; Namier, pp. 207–10.
229. McSherry, pp. 205–6.

of August 12, after a delay that could not help but cast Anglo-French intentions in the worst light, the military delegations had their first meeting and the Russians learned that the British attitude toward the negotiations was such that they did not even give their delegation written credentials to negotiate. On the same day, Astakhov received new instructions from Moscow authorizing him to tell Schnurre of the Soviet Government's interest in discussing the points raised by Schnurre two days before. Late on August 14, Ribbentrop instructed Schulenburg to press Moscow on the need for a nonaggression treaty "clarifying jointly territorial questions in Eastern Europe," and offered to travel to Moscow and meet with Stalin to secure the quickest possible settlement. On the morning of the 17th, Schulenburg presented Ribbentrop's message to Molotov, who responded that the trade agreement must first be signed, and that shortly thereafter a nonaggression pact with protocol defining the interests of each country could be concluded. The negotiations for the trade agreement were completed in Berlin on the evening of the 18th, and Stalin agreed to sign on the 19th. On the 20th Hitler urgently wired Stalin agreeing to Soviet terms for a nonaggression pact, with certain clarification; he insisted that Ribbentrop be received in Moscow within two days to conclude the treaty. On the 21st Stalin accepted Hitler's offer. Ribbentrop arrived in Moscow on the 23rd, where he was met by Molotov and Stalin. The negotiations went quickly and with ease, and a nonaggression pact was signed that day, including a special protocol granting Russia Bessarabia, Finland, Estonia, and part of Poland and Latvia. Now Hitler was free to go to war with Poland, which meant the start of World War II.

By all realistic standards, Stalin was justified in signing with Hitler as the best alternative at the time for the protection of Russia. What difference did it make to Stalin if this meant war for Britain and France? He was not interested in saving them from war, but rather in "diverting the conflagration away from Russia." Deutscher has written that to Stalin "the war was inevitable anyhow: if he had made no deal with Hitler, war would still have broken out either now or somewhat later, under conditions incomparably less favourable to his country." [230] It was Stalin who had consistently offered Russia's help to Britain and France in the event of war, and it was the Western Allies who rejected this help by refusing to agree to the terms on which it was offered, forcing Stalin to look elsewhere for protection and security. Britain's and France's conduct of every aspect of the negotiations in Moscow gave ample evidence that their real interest was not in securing a military alliance that could function in the event of war, but rather in gaining a greater measure of pressure in pursuit of an eventual agreement with Hitler, which was anathema to all legitimate Soviet interests and needs. Fontaine writes that Stalin "had no confidence in the Allies' intention. Their behavior during the military negotiations justified these doubts. At the end of August, he still had reason to believe that France and England would yield to the Hitlerian diktat, as they had the previous year." [231] The argument that Stalin could have chosen to remain neutral and refuse an agreement with Hitler because of its consequences is preposterous from the viewpoint of a Soviet leader concerned with guaranteeing his country's security to the best degree allowed by external circumstances. Faced with the attitude evidenced by Britain and France, Stalin was justified in accepting Hitler's offer as the best alternative. "He could not leave himself in a position of complete isolation in the face of the German attack on Poland," writes George Kennan.[232] As Churchill later wrote, Stalin's decision was "at the moment realistic in a high degree."[233] D. F. Fleming has summarized Russia's gains as a result of signing with Hitler:

> (1) They got everything in the Baltic States which the Allies had refused them, and more. . . . (2) They achieved freedom to correct their boundary with Finland and reclaim

230. Deutscher, p. 437.
231. Fontaine, p. 124.
232. Kennan, p. 309.
233. Churchill, p. 394.

Bessarabia from Rumania. (3) Instead of incurring the full power of the Nazi war machine, while the West viewed their plight with satisfaction, they turned Hitler back upon the West. (4) They also acquired nearly two years of precious time in which to prepare for a German onslaught.[234]

There can be no doubt that it was in Russia's interests to gain time in preparing for the inevitable conflict with Hitler. In response to the argument that the nonaggression pact also gave Hitler time and actually enabled him to build the forces required for a massive invasion of Russia, it must be pointed out that as of August 23, 1939, it did not seem possible that Hitler would be able to *increase* his strength once involved in war with at least Britain, France, and Poland. There is great validity in Churchill's assertion that "Stalin no doubt felt that Hitler would be a less deadly foe to Russia after a year of war with the Western Powers." [235]

234. Fleming pp. 96–97.
235. Churchill, p. 393.

Conclusion

In concluding this study, I would like to present a very brief framework in which the major points of the previous discussion may be related to the development of the Cold War.

The central point to be made is that at no time after the Bolshevik seizure of power in Russia was there the prospect that *a* cold war could be averted; given the realities of the situation, the mutual suspicions and fears, and the divergence of interests, there was really no chance for cooperation on a basis of mutual trust and faith. This is an observation that could be made about relations between any two sovereign states, but its significance is amplified in light of the enormous gulf that separated Soviet Russia from the West. This is not to say, however, that the manner in which the Cold War developed was inevitable. In analyzing the evolution of the Cold War, one must ask not "How could it have been averted at any given point?" but rather "How did specific events and decisions alter its contours, and what alternatives were available that might have changed the course of its development?"

As I have previously stated, the events from the Bolshevik revolution to 1936 laid the foundation on which the Cold War was subsequently waged, but their significance for understanding the development of the Cold War is limited, for there was nothing that happened in those years that made any subsequent event inevitable. In the two years following 1937, the Chamberlain Cabinet chose to pursue a policy that contributed significantly to Soviet Russia's untenable position in Europe, eventually forced Stalin into an agreement with Hitler, and had wide-ranging implications for the future contours of the Cold War.

It is true that most members of the Chamberlain Cabinet shared views on domestic and foreign policy that made appeasement the most appealing policy alternative to them. Yet each was quite aware of the alternative to appeasement, and each (with the exceptions of Eden and Duff Cooper, who resigned) consciously and, they felt, with good reason, rejected a policy of preparation for war entailing a greatly expanded armaments program and an alteration of the status quo in Europe that would have facilitated or recognized Soviet hegemony in Eastern Europe. At each crucial juncture, the Cabinet, strongly influenced by Chamberlain, deliberately limited its policy options to those which entailed accepting German predominance in Central and Eastern Europe, on the assumption that Hitler could be kept from making war. Finally awakened to the imminence of war in 1939, the Cabinet sought to guarantee that England would be spared the sacrifices of war by turning Hitler's war machine toward the East, away from Western Europe. They realized that Soviet assistance would be essential in fighting Hitler, but they connived to secure the promise of such assistance at no price, that is, to commit Russia to fight for the preservation of a status quo against her interests.

By 1937 Stalin faced an extremely difficult and dangerous situation in Europe. The heart of his problem lay in the great loss of territory in Eastern Europe that Russia suffered as a result of her departure from World War I. Now Russia's western frontier was strategically indefensible, bordered by a string of states whose hostility to the Soviet Government was virtually fanatical. Stalin was powerless to take unilateral action, and for at least two years he rested his hopes on some type of partnership with Britain and France in which the three nations would recognize their common interest in stopping Hitler and in which Russia might improve her untenable position and perhaps even regain hegemony in Eastern Europe. When Stalin offered to aid in the fight against Hitler, he made clear that he would not commit his country to war unless he could be assured that such a sacrifice would bring about a more favorable situation in Europe. Stalin probably never believed that Britain and France would be willing to grant him what he asked, but as of the summer of 1939, he had no alternative but to put his country's forces at the disposal of the West and ask what he felt to be a fitting and necessary price; he knew by mid-1939 that Britain and France were desperate for his help, whatever their motives, and this may have led him to believe that an agreement could eventually be reached. Yet, when Hitler finally offered so irresistible a deal to Stalin the Soviet leader simply could no longer conduct his diplomacy on the same basis—waiting for Britain and France to yield to the ever-growing pressure for a full alliance. In August 1939 Stalin got the best deal he could reasonably have expected for the time and in the circumstances.

The events of World War II and its immediate aftermath have been described in numerous studies of the Cold War, and I shall not describe them here. I hope that this study, which prefaces the post-1939 years, helps the student of the Cold War to view the events of those later years in a clearer context. That there would be basic conflicts between the United States and Russia after the war was inevitable. That the Cold War would develop as it did under President Truman was not inevitable, however. Against the background of the events described in this study and the fantastic losses suffered by Russia in the war, there can be no doubt that Stalin realized that his paramount aim must be to retain sufficient control of Eastern Europe that his country would never again be placed in the position it had been in. That he would insist on keeping Eastern Europe in his grip after the war was inevitable, and his determination to do so was doubtless fueled by the frustrated diplomacy of 1937–1939. The *manner* in which he would retain this control was not inevitable, and was shaped largely in response to the degree to which his aims were opposed by the United States.

It is difficult to speak with certainty of President Roosevelt's attitudes toward postwar Russian policy, for Roosevelt had never committed himself to long-range plans, preferring to make policy according to the needs of the moment, and he died before the end of the war. He understood that the key to stability and peace after the war involved cooperation, however difficult or strained, between the United States and Russia; his policy decisions during the war suggest that he was willing to go far in achieving such cooperation. There is reason to believe that he would have been willing to accept Soviet hegemony in Eastern Europe, provided that Stalin's excesses were curbed to the degree that they did not hopelessly limit Roosevelt's political maneuverability at home. Roosevelt must be understood within the highly political context in which he operated. He had to keep the Congress and the people in line if his policies were to succeed, and, unlike Woodrow Wilson (whose failures Roosevelt sought not to repeat), he was a master political manipulator and propagandist—an observation that I make without value judgment. Roosevelt's political position toward the end of the war was an extremely difficult one, for, if postwar cooperation with the Russians were to be achieved on the basis of Soviet predominance in Eastern Europe, a huge and powerful body of anti-Soviet opinion—from the public, to the Congress, to the President's own advisers—would have to be satisfied, and the democratic rhetoric that was used to justify our involvement in the war would have to be squared away with the anti-democratic realities of the postwar world. The task was one that would have taxed the abilities of even the shrewdest politician.

Harry Truman's feelings about the Russians were very different from Roosevelt's, and, also unlike FDR, Truman was very significantly influenced by his advisers, who immediately descended upon him and successfully urged a tough line against Soviet postwar aims. Within months after becoming President, he had assumed a belligerent stand toward the Russians and destroyed virtually any political foundation at home on which a policy of cooperation might have been waged. There seems to have been a direct correlation between the vehemence with which the Truman Administration promoted anti-Soviet feelings at home and opposed Soviet policy abroad, and the degree to which Stalin increased the firmness of his control over Eastern Europe.

Bibliography

Aster, Sidney. *1939: The Making of the Second World War.*
   New York, 1973.
Beloff, Max. *The Foreign Policy of Soviet Russia, 1929–1941.*
   London, 1949.
Birkenhead, The Earl of. *Halifax: The Life of Lord Halifax.*
   London, 1965.
Carr, E. H. *International Relations Between the Two World
   Wars, 1919–1939.* New York, 1947.
Churchill, Winston S. *The Gathering Storm.* Boston, 1948.
Colvin, Ian. *None So Blind: A British Diplomatic View of the
   Origins of World War II.* New York, 1965.
———. *The Chamberlain Cabinet.* London, 1971.
Craster, H. H. E., ed. *Speeches on Foreign Policy by Viscount
   Halifax.* London, 1940.
Dark, E. P. *The World Against Russia?* Sydney, Australia, 1948.
Davies, Joseph E. *Mission to Moscow.* New York, 1943.
Deutscher, Issac. *Stalin: A Political Biography.* London, 1949.
Dilks, David, ed. *The Diaries of Sir Alexander Cadogan, 1938–
   1945.* New York, 1972.
Documents on German Foreign Policy, 1918–1945. Series D,
   1948 ff.
Eden, Anthony (The Earl of Avon). *Facing the Dictators.* Boston,
   1962.

189

————. *The Reckoning*. Boston, 1965.

Eubank, Keith. *Munich*. Norman, Okla., 1963.

————. *The Origins of World War II*. New York, 1969.

Feiling, Keith. *The Life of Neville Chamberlain*. London, 1947.

Fleming, D. F. *The Cold War and Its Origins, 1917–1960*. New York, 1961.

Fontaine, André. *History of the Cold War*. New York, 1968.

Furnia, Arthur H. *The Diplomacy of Appeasement*. Washington, 1960.

Gafencu, Grigore. *Last Days of Europe*. New Haven, Conn., 1948.

George, Margaret. *The Warped Vision: British Foreign Policy, 1933–1939*. Pittsburgh, Pa., 1965.

Gilbert, Martin. *Roots of Appeasement*. New York, 1966.

————, and Gott, Richard. *The Appeasers*. London, 1963.

Halifax, Edward Frederick. *Fulness of Days*. London, 1957.

Harvey, John, ed. *The Diplomatic Diaries of Oliver Harvey, 1937–1940*. New York, 1970.

Henderson, Neville. *Failure of a Mission: Berlin, 1937–1939*. New York, 1940.

Hoare, Sir Samuel (Viscount Templewood). *Nine Troubled Years*. London, 1954.

Kennan, George F. *Russia and the West Under Lenin and Stalin*. New York, 1961.

Lafore, Laurence. *The End of Glory*. Philadelphia, 1970.

Litvinov, Maxim. *Against Aggression, Speeches*. New York, 1939.

MacLeod, Iain. *Neville Chamberlain*. London, 1961.

MacLeod, Col. Roderick. *The Ironside Diaries, 1937–1940*. London, 1962.

McSherry, James E. *Stalin, Hitler, and Europe*. Cleveland, Ohio, 1968.

Marzani, Carl. *We Can Be Friends: Origins of the Cold War*. New York, 1952.

Medlicott, W. N. *The Coming of War in 1939*. London, 1963.

Middlemas, Keith. *Diplomacy of Illusion: The British Government and Germany, 1937–39*. London, 1972.

Ministry for Foreign Affairs, Czechoslovakia and U.S.S.R. *New Documents on the History of Munich*. Prague, 1958.

Ministry of Foreign Affairs of the U.S.S.R. *Documents and Materials Relating to the Eve of the Second World War*. Moscow, 1948.

Mosley, Leonard. *On Borrowed Time: How World War II Began*. New York, 1969.

Muggeridge, Malcolm. *Ciano's Diplomatic Papers*. London, 1948.
Namier, L. B. *Diplomatic Prelude: 1938–1939*. London, 1948.
———. *Europe in Decay, 1936–1940*. London, 1950.
Parkinson, Roger. *Peace For Our Time*. New York: David Mc-
   Kay Co., Inc., 1971.
Pritt, D. N. *Must the War Spread?* London, 1940.
Ripka, Hubert. *Munich: Before and After*. London, 1939.
Rock, William R. *Appeasement on Trial*. 1966.
Rubinstein, Alvin Z. *The Foreign Policy of the Soviet Union*.
   New York, 1972.
Salvemini, Gaetano. *Prelude to World War II*. London, 1953.
Strang, Lord William. *The Moscow Negotiations, 1939*. London,
   1968.
Taylor, A. J. P. *The Origins of the Second World War*. New York,
   1966.
Thorne, Christopher. *The Approach of War, 1938–1939*. New
   York, 1967.
Toynbee, Arnold, ed. *The Eve of War, 1939*. London, 1958.
Ulam, Adam B. *Expansion and Coexistence: The History of
   Soviet Foreign Policy, 1917–67*. New York, 1968.
U.S. Department of State. *Foreign Relations of the United States
   for the Years 1938 and 1939*.
von Dirksen, Herbert. *Moscow, Tokyo, London*. London, 1951.
Welles, Sumner. *The Time For Decision*. New York, 1944.
Wheeler-Bennett, John W. *Munich: Prologue to Tragedy*. New
   York, 1963.
Woodward, E. L., ed. *Documents on British Foreign Policy,
   1919–1939*. London, Third Series.

Index